# Introduction

Welcome to **The Ultimate Ninja Dual Zone Air Fryer Cookbook UK 2024,** This cookbook is a culmination of over 1900 days of delicious and healthy culinary exploration, designed to be your go-to guide for mastering the art of air frying with the Ninja Dual Zone Air Fryer.

Whether you're just starting your air frying journey or you're an experienced home cook looking for new inspiration, this cookbook has something for everyone. With a collection of over 200 meticulously crafted recipes, we've covered everything from satisfying breakfasts to everyday favorites, mouthwatering poultry and beef dishes, tempting snacks, indulgent desserts, and more.

At the heart of this cookbook is the Ninja Dual Zone Air Fryer, a versatile kitchen appliance that has revolutionized the way we cook. With its innovative cooking technology and dual-zone functionality, the Ninja Dual Zone Air Fryer offers precise control and consistent results, allowing you to create culinary masterpieces with ease.

As you embark on this culinary adventure, remember that cooking is not just about following recipes—it's about creativity, experimentation, and the joy of sharing delicious meals with loved ones. So, fire up your Ninja Dual Zone Air Fryer, let your imagination soar, and get ready to embark on a flavorful journey that will delight your taste buds and elevate your cooking skills.

Here's to many more days of delicious and healthy cooking with your Ninja Dual Zone Air Fryer!

**Happy Cooking!**

## What is The Ninja Foodi Dual Zone Air Fryer?

- The Ninja Foodi Dual Zone Air Fryer is a versatile kitchen appliance that combines the functionality of an air fryer with the convenience of having two independent cooking zones. This innovative appliance allows you to cook two separate dishes simultaneously, each with its own temperature and cooking time settings, providing flexibility and convenience for meal preparation.

- The Dual Zone Air Fryer features a range of cooking functions beyond air frying, including roasting, baking, dehydrating, and more, allowing you to prepare a wide variety of dishes with ease. Its spacious cooking baskets and adjustable temperature and time settings make it suitable for cooking everything from crispy snacks to full meals.

- With its rapid air circulation technology, the Ninja Foodi Dual Zone Air Fryer cooks food quickly and evenly, producing crispy, golden results without the need for excessive oil. This makes it a healthier alternative to traditional frying methods while still delivering delicious and satisfying meals.

- The intuitive controls and easy-to-clean design make the Ninja Foodi Dual Zone Air Fryer a convenient and user-friendly appliance for both beginners and experienced cooks. Whether you're cooking for yourself or a crowd, this versatile kitchen gadget can help you create a wide range of recipes with minimal effort and maximum flavor.

## What makes Ninja Dual Zone Air Fryer Different?

- Two Independent Cooking Zones: The appliance is equipped with two separate cooking zones, allowing you to cook two different foods at the same time without flavors mixing or the need for multiple appliances.
- Six Cooking Functions: In addition to air frying, the Ninja Dual Zone Air Fryer offers functions for max crisp, roast, bake, dehydrate, and reheat, providing versatility for a wide range of recipes and cooking styles.
- Even and Rapid Cooking: With its high-speed air circulation, the air fryer cooks food quickly and evenly, resulting in crispy textures and delicious flavors without excessive oil.
- Large Capacity: The spacious cooking baskets provide ample room for preparing meals for the whole family or entertaining guests.
- Smart Finish Feature: This feature ensures that both zones finish cooking at the same time, making meal planning and prep much easier.
- Precise Temperature and Time Control: The appliance allows for precise control over cooking temperature and time, ensuring consistent results with a wide variety of recipes.
- Additionally, the Ninja Dual Zone Air Fryer offers independent temperature and cooking time controls for each zone. This allows you to customize the cooking settings according to the specific requirements of each food item.
- Easy to Clean: The non-stick surfaces and dishwasher-safe components make cleaning up after cooking a breeze.

# A BEGINNER'S GUIDE

### *Unboxing and Setup:*

- When unboxing your Ninja Dual Zone Air Fryer, carefully remove all packaging materials and accessories. Place the air fryer on a stable, flat surface with enough clearance around it for proper ventilation.
- Ensure the appliance is plugged into a suitable power outlet.

### *Getting to Know Your Air Fryer:*

- Familiarize yourself with the control panel and settings. The Ninja Dual Zone Air Fryer typically features a digital display and buttons for selecting cooking functions, time, and temperature.
- Take note of the different cooking functions available, such as air fry, max crisp, roast, bake, dehydrate, and reheat. Each function is designed for specific cooking needs.

### *Preparing for First Use:*

- Before using the air fryer for the first time, it's important to read the user manual thoroughly to understand its features, safety precautions, and maintenance instructions.
- Wash the cooking baskets, trays, and accessories with warm, soapy water and dry them thoroughly before use.

### *Tips for Successful Air Frying:*

- Preheat the air fryer if the recipe calls for it. Preheating helps ensure even cooking and better results.
- Use the recommended cooking temperature and time settings for the recipe you're preparing. Adjust as needed based on your preferences and experience.
- Arrange food items in a single layer in the cooking baskets to allow for proper air circulation and even cooking.
- Shake or flip the food halfway through the cooking process to ensure all sides are evenly cooked and crispy.

### *Cleaning and Maintenance:*

- After each use, allow the air fryer to cool down before cleaning.
- The cooking baskets, trays, and accessories are usually dishwasher safe. Alternatively, you can wash them with warm, soapy water and a non-abrasive sponge.
- Wipe the exterior of the air fryer with a damp cloth to remove any food residue or spills.

### *Experimenting with Recipes:*

- Start with simple recipes to familiarize yourself with the air fryer's cooking process and capabilities.
- As you become more comfortable, try experimenting with different ingredients, seasonings, and cooking techniques to create your own unique dishes.

### *Safety Precautions:*

- Always handle the air fryer with care, especially when it's hot.
- Keep the appliance away from water and other liquids to prevent electrical hazards.
- Follow all safety instructions provided in the user manual to ensure safe and proper use of the air fryer.

With this beginner's guide, you're ready to embark on your air frying journey with the Ninja Dual Zone Air Fryer. Enjoy exploring new recipes and discovering the endless possibilities of this versatile kitchen appliance!

# MORE THAN AN AIR FRYER

- **AIR FRY**– Up 70% less fat than traditional frying methods. Enjoy guilt-free fried favourites using little to no oil. From delicious chicken wings, fishcakes, burgers and sausages to chunky chips. Air frying evenly circulates super-hot air around food to remove excess moisture and give it a delicious golden finish.

- **ROAST** - Enjoy your favourite roast meat, fish and vegetables any day of the week. From salmon fillets, golden chicken breasts and roast pork chops with crispy crackling to fluffy roast potatoes, balsamic-roasted tomatoes and sweet potato hash.

- **MAX CRISP**– Cook from frozen to crispy in minutes. Temperatures of 240°C evenly cook and crisp your favourite frozen foods. From breaded scampi and chicken nuggets to golden French fries, onion rings and more. Perfect for quick, delicious dinners.

- **DEHYDRATE** - Create delicious dried fruit snacks, from apple to mango, banana to pineapple. Enjoy homemade vegetable crisps, beef jerky, and even make your own dried herbs.

- **BAKE** - Easily cook pasta bakes, fish pies and flaky fish with crispy toppings, or enjoy freshly-baked bread and homemade sweet treats, from muffins and brownies to cakes and cookies.

- **REHEAT** - Restore leftovers to that delicious fresh-out-of-the-oven finish, perfect for reviving leftover pizza, quiche, spring rolls and more.

- Variable temperature controls let you make every snack and meal just how you like it. The innovative Auto-Adjust Fan automatically changes speeds based on the cooking function selected.

- The easy-to-use digital control panel with a countdown timer makes it easy to see how much cooking time is left.

- Washing up is easy thanks to non-stick, dishwasher-safe parts.

We use the average capacity of Ninja Dual Zone Air Fryer models to write our recipes. Therefore, if one of the cooking instructions is for one zone but it doesn't fit in a single zone of your air fryer, divide it and cook it on two zones, and vice versa. The temperature and time still follow our provided formulas.

The MATCH button is frequently used to duplicate settings across both zones. However, don't forget about the SYNC button when you want to cook two separate dishes and serve them simultaneously.

# TABLE OF CONTENTS

|  | Introduction |
|---|---|
| 01 | **Breakfasts Recipes** |
| 14 | **Family Favorites** |
| 26 | **Fast & Easy Everyday** |
| 38 | **Poultry** |
| 51 | **Beef, Pork & Lamb** |
| 64 | **Fish & Seafood** |
| 77 | **Desserts** |
| 89 | **Snacks** |
| 98 | **Vegetarian Mains** |

Publishing black & white Cookbook without images aims to optimize the number of recipes and offer the lowest selling price to customers. In addition, it also contributes to protecting the environment from the harmful effects of color printing inks. Maybe some customers will prefer color printed books, in this case, we hope to receive your sympathy, we sincerely thank you!

## Breakfasts Recipes

- Hash Browns — 1
- Bacon & Egg Cups — 1
- Air-Fried Muffins — 2
- Black Pudding Sausages — 2
- Bubble & Squeak Patties — 3
- Crispy Air-Fried Cereal Bars — 3
- Pancakes with Maple Syrup — 4
- Air-Fried Tomatoes — 4
- Oatmeal Breakfast Cookies — 5
- Sweet Potato and Bacon Hash — 5
- Breakfast Calzone — 6
- Black Pudding Fritters — 6
- Breakfast Burritos — 7
- Blueberry Pancake Bites — 7
- Breakfast Sandwiches — 8
- Baked Beans on Toast — 8
- Porridge Bites — 9
- Banana Bread Muffins — 9
- Cinnamon Raisin Bagel Chips — 10
- Blueberry French Toast — 10
- Cranberry Orange Scones — 11
- Banana Fritters — 11
- Breakfast Tostadas — 12
- Coconut Pancakes — 12
- Breakfast Bruschetta — 13
- Morning Quiche — 13

## Family Favorites

- Fish and Chips — 14
- Chicken Nuggets — 14
- Cheese & Onion Pasties — 15
- Chicken Drumsticks — 15
- Vegetable Spring Rolls — 16
- Scotch Eggs — 16
- Homemade Chicken Burgers — 17
- Beef & Vegetable Pies — 17
- Stuffed Mushrooms — 18
- Pork Chops — 18
- Breaded Mozzarella Sticks — 19
- Potato Wedges — 19
- Vegetable Samosas — 20
- Air-Fried Lasagna Rolls — 20
- Mushroom Risotto Balls — 21
- Beef & Onion Sausages — 21
- Crispy Chicken Tenders — 22
- Cheesy Garlic Breadsticks — 22
- Prawn Spring Rolls — 23
- Chicken Quesadillas — 23
- Macaroni & Cheese Bites — 24
- Homemade Fish Fingers — 24
- Vegetarian Quesadillas — 25
- Sweet Potato Fries — 25

## Fast & Easy Everyday Favourites

- Quick Fish Fillets — 26
- Crispy Chicken Wings — 26
- Cheese & Ham Quesadillas — 27
- Easy Vegetable Fritters — 27
- Veggie Burgers — 28
- Avocado Fries — 28
- Zucchini Chips — 29
- Veggie Sticks — 29
- Swift Garlic Bread — 30
- Cheese Balls — 30
- Sweetcorn Fritters — 31
- Quick Pita Chips — 31
- Egg Rolls — 32
- Tofu Bites — 32
- Mediterranean Vegetables — 33
- Speedy Bacon — 33
- Rapid Shrimp — 34
- Garlic Parmesan Shrimp — 34
- Lemon Pepper Shrimp — 35

- Teriyaki Chicken — 35
- BBQ Chicken — 36
- Cheese-Walnut Stuffed Mushrooms — 36
- Potato with Creamy Cheese — 37
- Traditional Queso Fundido — 37

## **Poultry**

- Garlic Parmesan Chicken — 38
- Lemon Pepper Chicken Breasts — 38
- Teriyaki Chicken Skewers — 39
- Southern Fried Chicken — 39
- Buffalo Chicken Tenders — 40
- Herb-Crusted Turkey Wings — 40
- Soy Ginger Duck Breast — 41
- Crispy Quail — 41
- Orange Glazed Chicken — 42
- Maple Dijon Chicken Thighs — 42
- Peri-Peri Chicken — 43
- Sesame Ginger Chicken Wings — 43
- Pesto Parmesan Chicken — 44
- Spicy Sriracha Chicken — 44
- Lime & Cilantro Chicken — 45
- Garlic Butter Chicken Breast — 45
- Crispy Coconut Chicken Strips — 46
- Mango Chili Turkey Breast — 46
- Pesto Crusted Chicken — 47
- Thyme & Garlic Chicken — 47
- Tandoori Spiced Chicken — 48
- Sesame Soy Chicken Strips — 48
- Moroccan Spiced Turkey — 49
- Crispy Herbed Chicken Tenders — 49
- Chili Lime Turkey Breast — 50
- Honey Soy Chicken Drumsticks — 50

## **Beef, Pork & Lamb**

- Beef Burgers — 51
- Beef & Spinach Rolls — 51
- Beef Kebabs — 52
- Beef Meatballs — 52
- Beef Steak Bites — 53
- Corned Beef Hash Patties — 53
- Beef & Lamb Gyros — 54
- Beef Teriyaki Skewers — 54
- Beef Satay Skewers — 55
- BBQ Beef Ribs — 55
- Beef Fajitas — 56
- Pork Tenderloin — 56
- Pulled Pork Sliders — 57
- Pork Sausages — 57
- Pork Belly Bites — 58
- Pork Schnitzel Bites — 58
- Crispy Pork Carnitas — 59
- Pork Stir-Fried Rice — 59
- Lamb Chops — 60
- Lamb Kofta — 60
- Lamb Shawarma — 61
- Lamb Skewers — 61
- Lamb Meatballs — 62
- Mixed Grill Platter — 62
- Sausage Rolls — 63
- Meat Pies — 63

## **Fish & Seafood**

- Miso Glazed Black Cod — 64
- Fish Tacos — 64
- Prawn Tempura — 65
- Salmon Patties — 65
- Scampi — 66
- Air-fried Fish Fingers — 66
- Air-fried Sardines — 67
- Cajun Spiced Catfish — 67
- Crispy Haddock Bites — 68
- Lemon Garlic Butter Salmon — 68
- Teriyaki Glazed Salmon — 69
- Grilled Swordfish Skewers — 69
- Coconut Crusted Cod — 70

- Pesto-crusted Halibut — 70
- Spicy Grilled Mackerel — 71
- Herb-crusted Sea Bass — 71
- Coconut Shrimp — 72
- Smoked Paprika Shrimp — 72
- Garlic Butter Shrimp — 73
- Crispy Prawn Balls — 73
- Piri-piri Prawns — 74
- Cajun Shrimp Skewers — 74
- Spicy Cajun Crawfish — 75
- Tandoori Fish tikka — 75
- Beer battered Haddock — 76
- Salt & Pepper Squid — 76

## Desserts

- Apple Crisp — 77
- Banana Fritters — 77
- Bread Pudding — 78
- Brownies — 78
- Chocolate Chip Cookies — 79
- Churros — 79
- Cinnamon Rolls — 80
- Donuts — 80
- Eclairs — 81
- Fruit Crumble — 81
- Lemon Bars — 82
- Mini Cheesecakes — 82
- Peach Cobbler — 83
- Pineapple Upside-Down Cake — 83
- Shortbread Cookies — 84
- S'mores — 84
- Sticky Toffee Pudding — 85
- Strawberry Shortcake — 85
- Tiramisu — 86
- Vanilla Custard Tart — 86
- Carrot Cake — 87
- Chocolate Lava Cake — 87
- Lemon Drizzle Cake — 88
- Bakewell Tart — 88

## Snacks

- Crispy Air-Fried Potato Skins — 89
- Onion Rings — 89
- Buffalo Cauliflower Bites — 90
- Crispy Air-Fried Pickles — 90
- Cheddar & Bacon Potato Bites — 91
- Sesame Chicken Wontons — 91
- Crispy Crab Rangoon — 92
- Chickpea & Spinach Patties — 92
- Breaded Avocado Slices — 93
- Curry Puff Pastries — 93
- Crispy Air-Fried Okra — 94
- Garlic Herb Pita Chips — 94
- Crispy Cauliflower Wings — 95
- Prawn Toast — 95
- Samosas — 96
- Mozzarella Sticks — 96
- Jalapeño Poppers — 97
- Mini Pizzas — 97

## Vegetarian Mains

- Croutons — 98
- Falafel — 98
- Crispy Tofu Bites — 99
- Vegetarian Burger Patties — 99
- Super Vegetable Burger — 100
- Vegetarian Sausages — 100
- Zucchini Fritters — 101
- Cauliflower Wings — 101
- Aloo Tikki — 102
- Vegan Nuggets — 102
- Vegetable Tempura — 103
- Vegetable Stir-Fry — 103
- Stuffed Bell Peppers — 104
- Mushroom Skewers — 104
- Vegetarian Kebabs — 105
- Veggie Fritters — 105

# Hash Browns

🕐 **Cooking Time:** 20 Min  🍽 **Servings:** 8 hash browns

- 500g potatoes, peeled and grated
- 1 small onion, grated
- 2 tbsp all-purpose flour
- 1 tsp salt
- 1/2 tsp black pepper
- 2 tbsp vegetable oil

# Bacon & Egg Cups

🕐 **Cooking Time:** 12 Min  🍽 **Servings:** 8 Bacon & Egg Cups

- 8 slices of bacon
- 8 large eggs
- Salt and pepper to taste
- Fresh chives for garnish (optional)

## INSTRUCTION

**Hash Browns:**

1. Place the grated potatoes in a clean kitchen towel and squeeze out any excess moisture.
2. In a large bowl, combine the grated potatoes, grated onion, flour, salt, and black pepper. Mix until well combined.
3. Divide the potato mixture into 8 portions and shape each portion into a patty.
4. Brush both sides of each potato patty with vegetable oil.
5. Evenly dividing them between the two zone of the air fryer, ensuring they are arranged in a single layer.
6. Select Zone 1, choose the AIR FRY program, and set the temperature to 200°C. Set the time to 15-20 minutes.
7. Select MATCH to duplicate settings across both zones. Press the START/STOP button to begin cooking.
8. After 10 minutes, carefully flip the potato patties using a spatula to ensure even cooking.
9. Continue cooking for another 5-10 minutes or until the hash browns are golden brown and crispy.
10. Once cooked, remove the hash browns from the air fryer and place them on a plate lined with paper towels to drain any excess oil.
11. Serve the **hash browns** warm as a delicious side dish or breakfast item

**Bacon & Egg Cups:**

1. Lightly grease 8 cups of a muffin tin with oil or cooking spray.
2. Take a slice of bacon and line the sides of one muffin cup, forming a ring. Repeat with the remaining slices of bacon and muffin cups.
3. Crack an egg into each bacon-lined muffin cup.
4. Season each egg with salt and pepper to taste.
5. Evenly dividing them between the two zone of the air fryer, ensuring they are arranged in a single layer.
6. Select Zone 1, choose the BAKE program, and set the temperature to 180°C. Set the time to 10-12 minutes.
7. Select MATCH to duplicate settings across both zones. Press the START/STOP button to begin cooking
8. Check the bacon and egg cups after 10 minutes to see if the eggs are cooked to your liking and the bacon is crispy. If not, cook for an additional 1-2 minutes.
9. Once cooked, carefully remove the muffin tin from the air fryer.
10. Use a spoon to gently lift each **bacon and egg cup** out of the muffin tin.
11. Garnish with fresh chives if desired and serve immediately.

## Air-Fried Muffins

🕐 **Cooking Time:** 20 Min   🍴 **Servings:** 12 muffins

- 200g all-purpose flour
- 100g granulated sugar
- 1 tsp baking powder
- 1/2 tsp baking soda
- 1/4 tsp salt
- 1 large egg
- 120ml milk
- 60ml vegetable oil
- 1 tsp vanilla extract
- Optional: Add-ins such as chocolate chips, blueberries, or chopped nuts

## Black Pudding Sausages

🕐 **Cooking Time:** 15 Min   🍴 **Servings:** 4-6 sausages

- 250g black pudding, casing removed and crumbled
- 250g pork sausage meat
- 1 small onion, finely chopped
- 1 garlic clove, minced
- 1 tbsp fresh parsley, chopped
- 1 tsp dried sage
- Salt and pepper to taste
- Vegetable oil for frying

## INSTRUCTION

1. In a large mixing bowl, whisk together the flour, sugar, baking powder, baking soda, and salt.
2. In another bowl, whisk together the egg, milk, vegetable oil, and vanilla extract until well combined.
3. Pour the wet ingredients into the dry ingredients and stir until just combined. Be careful not to overmix.
4. If using any add-ins such as chocolate chips, blueberries, or chopped nuts, gently fold them into the batter.
5. Line a muffin tin with paper liners or grease the wells with oil. Spoon the muffin batter into the prepared muffin tin, filling each well about 2/3 full.
6. Evenly dividing them between the two zone of the air fryer, ensuring they are arranged in a single layer.
7. Select Zone 1, choose the BAKE program, and set the temperature to 180°C. Set the time to 15-18 minutes. Select MATCH. Press the START/STOP button to begin cooking.
8. Check the muffins after 15 minutes with a toothpick inserted into the center of a muffin coming out clean. If not, cook for an additional 2-3 minutes.
9. Once cooked through and golden brown, carefully remove the **muffins** from the air fryer and let them cool slightly. Serve the air-fried muffins warm or at room temperature.

1. In a large mixing bowl, combine the crumbled black pudding, pork sausage meat, chopped onion, minced garlic, chopped parsley, dried sage, salt, and pepper. Mix well until all the ingredients are evenly distributed.
2. Take a small portion of the mixture and shape it into a sausage shape, about 8-10cm long and 2-3cm thick. Repeat with the remaining mixture to form the sausages.
3. Lightly grease the air fryer basket with vegetable oil. Place the black pudding sausages in Zone 1 of the air fryer basket, ensuring they are not overcrowded.
4. Select Zone 1, choose the AIR FRY program, and set the temperature to 180°C. Set the time to 12-15 minutes. Press the START/STOP button to begin cooking.
5. After 6-8 minutes, carefully turn the sausages over using tongs to ensure even cooking.
6. Continue cooking for another 6-7 minutes or until the sausages are cooked through and golden brown.
7. Once cooked, remove the **sausages** from the air fryer and let them cool slightly before serving.

## Bubble & Squeak Patties

🕐 **Cooking Time:** 15 Min  🍴 **Servings:** 4-6 patties

- 500g potatoes, peeled and roughly chopped
- 250g cabbage, finely shredded
- 1 small onion, finely chopped
- 1-2 tbsp butter
- Salt and pepper to taste
- Vegetable oil for frying

## Crispy Air-Fried Cereal Bars

🕐 **Cooking Time:** 8 Min  🍴 **Servings:** 12 cereal bars

- 120g marshmallows
- 50g unsalted butter
- 150g crispy rice cereal (e.g., Rice Krispies)
- 50g milk chocolate chips
- 1 tbsp vegetable oil
- Optional: sprinkles, chopped nuts, dried fruit for topping.

---

## INSTRUCTION

---

1. Boil the potatoes in a large pot of salted water until tender, about 15-20 minutes. Drain well and return them to the pot.
2. While the potatoes are boiling, steam or boil the shredded cabbage until it is just tender, about 5-7 minutes. Drain well.
3. In a frying pan, melt the butter over medium heat. Add the chopped onion and cook until softened and translucent, about 5 minutes.
4. Add the cooked cabbage to the frying pan with the onions and continue to cook for another 2-3 minutes, stirring occasionally. Season with salt and pepper to taste.
5. Mash the boiled potatoes in the pot until smooth and creamy. Add the cooked cabbage and onion mixture to the mashed potatoes. Mix well to combine all the ingredients.
6. Using your hands, shape the mixture into patties, about 2-3 inches in diameter and 1/2 inch thick.
7. Lightly grease the air fryer basket with vegetable oil.
8. Place the Bubble and Squeak Patties in Zone 1 of the air fryer basket, ensuring they are not overcrowded.
9. Select Zone 1, choose the AIR FRY program, and set the temperature to 180°C. Set the time to 12-15 minutes. Press the START/STOP.
10. After 6-8 minutes, carefully turn the patties over using tongs to ensure even cooking.
11. Continue cooking for another 6-7 minutes or until the patties are golden brown and crispy.
12. Once cooked, remove the **patties** from the air fryer and let them cool slightly before serving.

1. In a large microwave-safe bowl, microwave the marshmallows and unsalted butter in 30-second intervals until melted and smooth.
2. Add the crispy rice cereal to the melted marshmallow mixture and stir until evenly coated.
3. Line a baking pan with parchment paper and press the cereal mixture into the pan.
4. Place the pan in Zone 1 of the air fryer basket.
5. Select Zone 1, choose the BAKE program, and set the temperature to 160°C. Set the time to 6-8 minutes. Press the START/STOP.
6. After 3-4 minutes, carefully flip the cereal bar using a spatula.
7. Continue cooking for another 3-4 minutes or until golden brown and crispy.
8. Remove the pan from the air fryer and let the cereal bars cool.
9. In a microwave-safe bowl, microwave the chocolate chips and vegetable oil in 30-second intervals until melted.
10. Drizzle the melted chocolate over the cooled cereal bars and add optional toppings.
11. Allow the chocolate to set before cutting the cereal **bars** into squares or rectangles.
12. Serve and enjoy!

# Pancakes with Maple Syrup

🕐 **Cooking Time:** 8  Min   🍴 **Servings:** 6-8 pancakes

- 150g all-purpose flour
- 2 tbsp granulated sugar
- 1 tsp baking powder
- 1/2 tsp baking soda
- Pinch of salt
- 1 large egg
- 180ml buttermilk
- 30ml vegetable oil
- Maple syrup for serving
- Butter for greasing

# Air-Fried Tomatoes

🕐 **Cooking Time:** 8  Min   🍴 **Servings:** 2

- 2 large tomatoes
- 1-2 tbsp olive oil
- Salt and pepper to taste
- Optional: garlic powder, dried herbs (e.g., thyme, basil, oregano)

## INSTRUCTION

1. In a mixing bowl, whisk together the all-purpose flour, granulated sugar, baking powder, baking soda, and a pinch of salt.
2. In another bowl, beat the egg, then add the buttermilk and vegetable oil. Mix until well combined.
3. Gradually pour the wet ingredients into the dry ingredients, stirring until just combined. Be careful not to overmix; the batter should be slightly lumpy.
4. Lightly grease the air fryer basket with butter.
5. Spoon the pancake batter into the air fryer basket, evenly dividing them between the two zone of the air fryer, forming pancakes of your desired size. Leave some space between each pancake for even cooking.
6. Select Zone 1, choose the BAKE program, and set temperature to 180°C, time to 4-5 minutes. Select MATCH. Press the START/STOP button to begin cooking.
7. After 2-3 minutes, carefully flip the pancakes using a spatula to ensure even cooking.
8. Continue cooking for another 2-3 minutes or until the pancakes are golden brown and cooked through.
9. Once cooked, remove the **pancakes** from the air fryer and serve them warm **with maple syrup**.

1. Wash the tomatoes and pat them dry with a paper towel.
2. Cut the tomatoes into thick slices, about 1.3 cm (1/2 inch) thick.
3. In a bowl, drizzle the tomato slices with olive oil and season with salt, pepper, and any optional seasonings to taste. Toss gently to coat.
4. Place the seasoned tomato slices in Zone 1 of the air fryer basket, ensuring they are not too crowded to allow for even cooking.
5. Select Zone 1, choose the AIR FRY program, and set the temperature to 200°C. Set the time to 6-8 minutes.
6. Press the START/STOP button to begin cooking.
7. After 3-4 minutes, carefully flip the tomato slices using tongs to ensure even cooking.
8. Continue cooking for another 3-4 minutes or until the tomatoes are tender and slightly charred on the edges.
9. Once cooked, remove the **tomatoes** from the air fryer and serve them as a side dish or as part of a meal.

# Oatmeal Breakfast Cookies

⏰ **Cooking Time: 10 Min** 🍴 **Servings: 12 cookies**

- 100g rolled oats
- 60g whole wheat flour
- 60g dried fruit (raisins, cranberries, chopped dates,,,)
- 30g chopped nuts (walnuts, almonds, pecans, etc.)
- 60ml honey or maple syrup
- 60g unsalted butter, melted
- 1 large egg
- 1/2 tsp vanilla extract
- 1/2 tsp ground cinnamon
- 1/4 tsp baking soda
- Pinch of salt

# Sweet Potato & Bacon Hash

⏰ **Cooking Time: 15 Min** 🍴 **Servings: 4**

- 2 large sweet potatoes, peeled and diced
- 200g bacon, diced
- 1 small onion, diced
- 1 bell pepper, diced
- 2 cloves garlic, minced
- 1 tsp paprika
- 1/2 tsp dried thyme
- Salt and pepper to taste
- 2 tbsp olive oil

## INSTRUCTION

1. In a large mixing bowl, combine the rolled oats, whole wheat flour, dried fruit, chopped nuts, ground cinnamon, baking soda, and a pinch of salt. Mix well to combine.
2. In a separate bowl, whisk together the melted butter, honey or maple syrup, egg, and vanilla extract until smooth.
3. Pour the wet ingredients into the dry ingredients and stir until everything is well combined and forms a dough.
4. Line the air fryer baskets with parchment paper.
5. Scoop about 2 tablespoons of dough and shape it into a ball. Place it on the lined air fryer basket and flatten it slightly with your fingers to form a cookie shape. Repeat with the remaining dough, leaving some space between the cookies.
6. Evenly dividing them between the two zone of the air fryer, ensuring they are arranged in a single layer.
7. Select Zone 1, choose the BAKE program, and set the temperature to 180°C. Set the time to 8-10 minutes. Select MATCH. Press the START/STOP.
8. After 4-5 minutes, carefully flip the cookies using a spatula to ensure even cooking.
9. Continue cooking for another 4-5 minutes or until the cookies are golden brown and firm to the touch.
10. Once cooked, remove the cookies from the air fryer and let them cool on a wire rack.
11. Serve the **oatmeal breakfast cookies** as a wholesome and delicious breakfast.

1. In a large bowl, toss the diced sweet potatoes with 1 tablespoon of olive oil, paprika, dried thyme, salt, and pepper until evenly coated.
2. Place the seasoned sweet potatoes in Zone 1 of the air fryer basket, ensuring they are spread out in a single layer.
3. Select Zone 1, choose the AIR FRY program, and set the temperature to 200°C. Set the time to 15 minutes.
4. Press the START/STOP button to begin cooking.
5. In the meantime, heat the remaining olive oil in a skillet over medium heat. Add the diced bacon and cook until crisp.
6. Add the diced onion, bell pepper, and minced garlic to the skillet with the bacon. Sauté until the vegetables are tender.
7. Once the sweet potatoes in the air fryer are halfway through cooking (after about 7-8 minutes), carefully remove the basket and add the cooked bacon, onion, bell pepper, and garlic mixture to Zone 1 of the air fryer basket.
8. Gently toss everything together in the air fryer basket to combine.
9. Continue cooking for the remaining time or until the sweet potatoes are tender and lightly browned, and the bacon is crispy.
10. Once cooked, remove the **sweet potato and bacon hash** from the air fryer and serve hot.

## Breakfast Calzone

🕐 **Cooking Time: 15 Min**   🍴 **Servings: 2**

- 1 sheet of ready-made pizza dough
- 4 large eggs
- 100g cooked breakfast sausage, crumbled
- 50g shredded cheddar cheese
- 50g diced bell peppers
- Salt and pepper to taste
- Olive oil for brushing

## Black Pudding Fritters

🕐 **Cooking Time: 12 Min**   🍴 **Servings: 4**

- 250g black pudding, casing removed and crumbled
- 1 large egg
- 50g plain flour
- 50g breadcrumbs
- 1 tsp dried mixed herbs (optional)
- Salt and pepper to taste
- Olive oil or cooking spray for greasing

---

## INSTRUCTION

1. Roll out the pizza dough on a lightly floured surface into a rectangle shape, about 1/4 inch thick.
2. In a bowl, whisk the eggs and season with salt and pepper.
3. Spread the scrambled eggs evenly over half of the pizza dough, leaving a border around the edges.
4. Sprinkle the crumbled breakfast sausage, shredded cheddar cheese, and diced bell peppers over the eggs.
5. Fold the other half of the dough over the filling to create a half-moon shape. Press the edges firmly to seal.
6. Lightly brush the calzone with olive oil.
7. Place the calzone in Zone 1 of the air fryer basket, ensuring it is not too close to the edges.
8. Select Zone 1, choose the AIR FRY program, and set the temperature to 200°C. Set the time to 12-15 minutes.
9. Press the START/STOP button to begin cooking.
10. After 6-8 minutes, carefully flip the calzone using a spatula to ensure even cooking.
11. Continue cooking for another 6-7 minutes or until the calzone is golden brown and crispy.
12. Once cooked, remove the calzone from the air fryer and let it cool for a few minutes before slicing.
13. Serve the **breakfast calzone** warm with your favorite breakfast condiments or sauces.

1. In a mixing bowl, combine the crumbled black pudding, egg, plain flour, breadcrumbs, dried mixed herbs (if using), salt, and pepper. Mix until well combined.
2. Divide the mixture into equal portions and shape each portion into a small round fritter.
3. Lightly grease the air fryer basket with olive oil or cooking spray.
4. Place the black pudding fritters in Zone 1 of the air fryer basket, ensuring they are not too close together.
5. Select Zone 1, choose the AIR FRY program, and set the temperature to 200°C. Set the time to 10-12 minutes.
6. Press the START/STOP button to begin cooking.
7. After 5-6 minutes, carefully flip the fritters using tongs to ensure even cooking.
8. Continue cooking for another 5-6 minutes or until the fritters are crispy and golden brown.
9. Once cooked, remove the fritters from the air fryer and let them cool slightly before serving.
10. Serve the **black pudding fritters** as a delicious appetizer or snack.

# Breakfast Burritos

🕐 **Cooking Time: 8**  Min   🍴 **Servings: 4**

- 4 large flour tortillas
- 4 large eggs
- 100g cooked breakfast sausage, crumbled
- 50g shredded cheddar cheese
- 1 small bell pepper, diced
- 50 g diced onions
- Salt and pepper to taste
- Olive oil or cooking spray for greasing

# Blueberry Pancake Bites

🕐 **Cooking Time: 6**  Min   🍴 **Servings: 12 pancake bites**

- 125g all-purpose flour
- 15g granulated sugar
- 5g baking powder
- 2.5g baking soda
- Pinch of salt
- 120ml buttermilk
- 1 large egg
- 30g unsalted butter, melted
- 75g fresh blueberries
- Maple syrup for serving

## INSTRUCTION

1. In a bowl, whisk the eggs and season with salt and pepper.
2. Heat a skillet over medium heat and add a little olive oil. Pour in the whisked eggs and scramble them until just set.
3. Lay out the flour tortillas on a clean surface. Divide the scrambled eggs, crumbled breakfast sausage, shredded cheddar cheese, diced bell pepper, and diced onions evenly among the tortillas, placing the fillings in the center of each tortilla.
4. Fold the sides of the tortillas over the fillings, then roll them up tightly to form burritos.
5. Lightly grease the air fryer basket with olive oil or cooking spray.
6. Place the breakfast burritos in Zone 1 of the air fryer basket, ensuring they are not too close together.
7. Select Zone 1, choose the AIR FRY program, and set the temperature to 180°C. Set the time to 6-8 minutes. Press the START/STOP.
8. After 3-4 minutes, carefully flip the burritos using tongs to ensure even cooking.
9. Continue cooking for another 3-4 minutes or until the burritos are golden brown and crispy.
10. Once cooked, remove the breakfast burritos from the air fryer and let them cool slightly before serving. Serve the **breakfast burritos** with your favorite salsa, hot sauce, or toppings

1. In a large bowl, whisk together the flour, sugar, baking powder, baking soda, and salt.
2. In another bowl, whisk the buttermilk, egg, and melted butter until well combined.
3. Pour the wet ingredients into the dry ingredients and mix until just combined. Be careful not to overmix.
4. Gently fold in the fresh blueberries.
5. Lightly grease the air fryer basket with cooking spray.
6. Spoon the pancake batter into the air fryer basket, filling each compartment about 2/3 full.
7. Place the basket in Zone 1 of the air fryer. Select Zone 1, choose the BAKE program, and set the temperature to 180°C. Set the time to 5-6 minutes.
8. Press the START/STOP button to begin cooking.
9. After 3-4 minutes, carefully flip the pancake bites using tongs to ensure even cooking.
10. Continue cooking for another 2-3 minutes or until the pancake bites are golden brown and cooked through.
11. Once cooked, remove the pancake bites from the air fryer and let them cool slightly before serving.
12. Serve the **blueberry pancake bites** warm with maple syrup for dipping.

## Breakfast Sandwiches

🕐 **Cooking Time:** 8 Min  🍴 **Servings:** 4 sandwiches

- 4 English muffins, split
- 4 large eggs
- 4 slices of cooked bacon or breakfast sausage patties
- 4 slices of cheese (cheddar, American, or your choice)
- Salt and pepper to taste
- Butter for greasing

## Baked Beans on Toast

🕐 **Cooking Time:** 6 Min  🍴 **Servings:** 4

- 400g can of baked beans
- 4 slices of bread (white, wholemeal, or your choice)
- Butter for spreading (optional)
- Salt and pepper to taste
- Grated cheese (optional, for topping)

---

## INSTRUCTION

---

1. Lightly grease the air fryer basket with butter.
2. Crack two egg into each compartment of the air fryer basket. Season with salt and pepper to taste. Select Zone 1, choose the AIR FRY program, set the temperature to 180°C. Set time to 4-5 minutes for soft-cooked eggs or 6-7 minutes for hard-cooked eggs. Select MATCH. Press the START/STOP
3. While the eggs are cooking, split the English muffins.
4. Once the eggs are cooked to your desired doneness, remove the basket from the air fryer.
5. Assemble the breakfast sandwiches by placing a slice of cheese on the bottom half of each English muffin. Top with a cooked egg and a slice of bacon or a breakfast sausage patty.
6. Evenly dividing the assembled sandwiches between the two zone.
7. Select Zone 1, choose the AIR FRY program, and set the temperature to 180°C. Set the time to 2-3 minutes to melt the cheese and warm the sandwiches. Select MATCH. Press the START/STOP
8. Once the cheese is melted and the **sandwiches** are warmed through, remove them from the air fryer and Serve immediately.

1. Heat the baked beans in a saucepan over medium heat until hot, stirring occasionally.
2. Lightly toast the bread slices in a toaster or using the air fryer.
3. If desired, spread butter on the toasted bread slices. Then place the toasted bread slices in Zone 1 of the air fryer basket.
4. Select Zone 1, choose the AIR FRY program, and set the temperature to 180°C. Set the time to 2-3 minutes to warm the bread. Press the START/STOP.
5. Once the bread is warmed through, remove the basket from the air fryer.
6. Spoon the hot baked beans over the toasted bread slices.
7. Season with salt and pepper to taste.
8. If desired, sprinkle grated cheese over the baked beans.
9. Place the assembled baked beans on toast back in the air fryer basket and return the basket to Zone 1 of the air fryer.
10. Select Zone 1, choose the AIR FRY program, and set the temperature to 180°C. Set the time to 1-2 minutes to melt the cheese (if using) and heat the beans.
11. Once the cheese is melted (if using) and the beans are heated through, remove the baked beans on toast from the air fryer.
12. Serve the **baked beans on toast** immediately.

# Porridge Bites

⏱ **Cooking Time:** 12 Min  🍴 **Servings:** 12 porridge bites

- 100 g rolled oats
- 1 ripe banana, mashed
- 120 ml milk (dairy or plant-based)
- 1 tbsp honey or maple syrup (optional)
- 1/2 tsp ground cinnamon
- 1/4 tsp vanilla extract
- Pinch of salt
- Toppings of your choice (e.g., berries, nuts, seeds, chocolate chips)

# Banana Bread Muffins

⏱ **Cooking Time:** 18 Min  🍴 **Servings:** 8-10 muffins

- 2 ripe bananas, mashed
- 120g all-purpose flour
- 50g granulated sugar
- 1 tsp baking powder
- 1/2 tsp baking soda
- 1/4 tsp salt
- 1 large egg
- 60ml vegetable oil or melted butter
- 1/2 tsp vanilla extract
- Optional add-ins: chopped nuts, chocolate chips, dried fruit

---

## INSTRUCTION

---

1. In a mixing bowl, combine the rolled oats, mashed banana, milk, honey or maple syrup (if using), ground cinnamon, vanilla extract, and a pinch of salt. Mix well to combine.
2. Line the air fryer basket with parchment paper.
3. Spoon the porridge mixture into the air fryer basket, dividing it into equal portions to form bite-sized rounds. Leave some space between each portion for even cooking.
4. Add your desired toppings to each porridge bite, pressing them gently into the mixture.
5. Place the basket in Zone 1 of the air fryer. Select Zone 1, choose the BAKE program, and set the temperature to 180°C. Set the time to 10-12 minutes.
6. Press the START/STOP button to begin cooking.
7. After 5-6 minutes, carefully flip the porridge bites using a spatula to ensure even cooking.
8. Continue cooking for another 5-6 minutes or until the porridge bites are golden brown and firm.
9. Once cooked, remove the porridge bites from the air fryer and let them cool slightly before serving.
10. Serve the **porridge bites** as a delicious and portable breakfast or snack.

1. In a mixing bowl, combine the mashed bananas, egg, vegetable oil or melted butter, and vanilla extract. Mix well.
2. In another bowl, whisk together the all-purpose flour, granulated sugar, baking powder, baking soda, and salt.
3. Gradually add the dry ingredients to the wet ingredients, mixing until just combined. Be careful not to overmix.
4. If using any optional add-ins, gently fold them into the batter.
5. Line the air fryer basket with paper liners or lightly grease it with cooking spray.
6. Spoon the batter into the muffin liners, filling each about 3/4 full.
7. Evenly dividing them between the two zone of the air fryer.
8. Select Zone 1, choose the BAKE program, and set the temperature to 180°C. Set the time to 15-18 minutes. Select MATCH. Press the START/STOP button to begin cooking.
9. After 8-10 minutes, rotate the muffin tin for even cooking. Continue cooking for another 5-8 minutes or until a toothpick inserted into the center of a muffin comes out clean.
10. Once cooked, remove the muffins from the air fryer and let them cool in the tin for a few minutes before transferring them to a wire rack to cool completely. Serve **banana bread muffins**.

# Cinnamon Raisin Bagel Chips

🕐 **Cooking Time: 8   Min**   🍴 **Servings: 32 bagel chips**

- 2 cinnamon raisin bagels
- 2 tbsp melted butter
- 2 tbsp granulated sugar
- 1 tsp ground cinnamon

# Blueberry French Toast

🕐 **Cooking Time: 8   Min**   🍴 **Servings: 2**

- 4 slices of bread (white, wholemeal, or your choice)
- 2 large eggs
- 60ml milk (dairy or plant-based)
- 1/2 tsp ground cinnamon
- 1/2 tsp vanilla extract
- 50g fresh blueberries
- Maple syrup for serving
- Butter or cooking spray for greasing

## INSTRUCTION

1. Slice the cinnamon raisin bagels into thin rounds, about 1/4 inch thick.
2. Evenly dividing them in a single layer between the two zone of the air fryer.
3. Select Zone 1, choose the AIR FRY program, and set the temperature to 180°C. Set the time to 6-8 minutes. Select MATCH. Press the START/STOP.
4. While the bagel rounds are cooking, mix the granulated sugar and ground cinnamon in a small bowl.
5. After 3-4 minutes, carefully flip the bagel rounds using tongs to ensure even cooking.
6. Continue cooking for another 3-4 minutes or until the bagel rounds are golden brown and crisp.
7. Once cooked, remove the bagel chips from the air fryer and brush them with melted butter while they are still warm.
8. Sprinkle the cinnamon sugar mixture over the bagel chips, coating them evenly.
9. Let the **bagel chips** cool for a few minutes before serving.

1. In a shallow bowl, whisk together the eggs, milk, ground cinnamon, and vanilla extract until well combined.
2. Dip each slice of bread into the egg mixture, ensuring it is coated on both sides.
3. Lightly grease the air fryer basket with butter or cooking spray.
4. Place the dipped bread slices in Zone 1 of the air fryer basket, ensuring they are not too close together.
5. Select Zone 1, choose the AIR FRY program, and set the temperature to 180°C. Set the time to 6-8 minutes.
6. Press the START/STOP button to begin cooking.
7. After 3-4 minutes, carefully flip the French toast slices using tongs to ensure even cooking.
8. Sprinkle the fresh blueberries over the French toast slices.
9. Continue cooking for another 3-4 minutes or until the French toast is golden brown and cooked through.
10. Once cooked, remove the French toast from the air fryer.
11. Serve the **blueberry French toast** warm, drizzled with maple syrup.

# Cranberry Orange Scones

⏱ **Cooking Time:** 15 Min  🍴 **Servings:** 8 scones

- 225g all-purpose flour
- 50g granulated sugar
- 1 tbsp baking powder
- 1/4 tsp salt
- 85g unsalted butter, chilled and cut into small cubes
- Zest of 1 orange
- 60ml fresh orange juice
- 60ml milk
- 1 large egg
- 75g dried cranberries
- 1-2 tbsp milk (for brushing)
- Optional: coarse sugar for sprinkling

# Banana Fritters

⏱ **Cooking Time:** 10 Min  🍴 **Servings:** 12 banana fritters

- 3 ripe bananas
- 100g all-purpose flour
- 25g granulated sugar
- 1/2 tsp baking powder
- 1/4 tsp ground cinnamon
- Pinch of salt
- 1 large egg
- 60ml milk
- 1/2 tsp vanilla extract
- Cooking oil spray

## INSTRUCTION

1. In a large bowl, whisk together the flour, sugar, baking powder, and salt.
2. Add the chilled butter cubes to the dry ingredients. Using your fingers or a pastry cutter, rub the butter into the flour mixture until it resembles coarse crumbs.
3. Stir in the orange zest and dried cranberries.
4. In a separate bowl, whisk together the fresh orange juice, milk, and egg.
5. Pour the wet ingredients into the dry ingredients, and gently mix until the dough comes together. Be careful not to overmix.
6. Turn the dough out onto a lightly floured surface and pat it into a circle about 1-inch thick.
7. Use a sharp knife to cut the circle into 8 equal wedges.
8. Place the scones in Zone 1 of the air fryer basket, ensuring they are not too close together.
9. Brush the tops of the scones with a little milk and sprinkle with coarse sugar if desired.
10. Place the basket in Zone 1 of the air fryer. Select Zone 1, choose the BAKE program, and set the temperature to 180°C, time to 12-15 minutes. Press the START/STOP.
11. After 6-8 minutes, rotate the basket for even cooking.
12. Once cooked, remove the **scones** from the air fryer and let them cool on a wire rack. And Serve.

1. In a bowl, mash the ripe bananas until smooth.
2. In another bowl, whisk together the all-purpose flour, granulated sugar, baking powder, ground cinnamon, and a pinch of salt.
3. In a separate bowl, beat the egg and then add the milk and vanilla extract. Mix well.
4. Combine the wet ingredients with the dry ingredients and mix until smooth.
5. Dip each banana slice into the batter, coating it completely.
6. Lightly spray the air fryer basket with cooking oil spray.
7. Evenly dividing them in between the two zone of the air fryer, ensuring they are not too close together.
8. Select Zone 1, choose the AIR FRY program, set temperature to 180°C, time to 8-10 minutes. Select MATCH. Press the START/STOP.
9. After 4-5 minutes, carefully flip the banana fritters using tongs to ensure even cooking.
10. Continue cooking for another 4-5 minutes or until the fritters are golden brown and crispy.
11. Once cooked, remove the **banana fritters** from the air fryer and let them cool slightly before serving.

## Breakfast Tostadas

🕐 **Cooking Time:** 5 Min  🍴 **Servings:** 4 breakfast tostadas

- 4 corn tortillas
- 4 large eggs
- 1 avocado, sliced
- 200g cooked black beans
- 100g shredded cheddar cheese
- 1 tomato, diced
- 5 g chopped cilantro
- Salt and pepper to taste
- Olive oil or cooking spray for greasing

## Coconut Pancakes

🕐 **Cooking Time:** 5 Min  🍴 **Servings:** 6-8 pancakes

- 150g all-purpose flour
- 30g desiccated coconut
- 2 tbsp granulated sugar
- 1 tsp baking powder
- 1/2 tsp baking soda
- Pinch of salt
- 1 large egg
- 180ml coconut milk
- 60ml water
- 1/2 tsp vanilla extract
- Butter or cooking oil spray for greasing

## INSTRUCTION

1. Lightly grease the air fryer basket with olive oil or cooking spray.
2. Place the corn tortillas in Zone 1 of the air fryer basket, ensuring they are not too close together.
3. Select Zone 1, choose the AIR FRY program, and set the temperature to 180°C. Set the time to 4-5 minutes.
4. Press the START/STOP button to begin cooking.
5. While the tortillas are cooking, heat the black beans in a saucepan over medium heat until heated through.
6. In a separate skillet, cook the eggs to your desired doneness (e.g., fried, scrambled).
7. Once the tortillas are crisp, remove them from the air fryer and place them on serving plates.
8. Spread a layer of heated black beans on each tortilla.
9. Top each tostada with a cooked egg.
10. Sprinkle shredded cheddar cheese over the eggs.
11. Garnish with sliced avocado, diced tomato, and chopped cilantro.
12. Season with salt and pepper to taste.
13. Serve the **breakfast tostadas** immediately for a delicious and satisfying breakfast.

1. In a mixing bowl, whisk together the all-purpose flour, desiccated coconut, granulated sugar, baking powder, baking soda, and a pinch of salt.
2. In another bowl, beat the egg, then add the coconut milk, water, and vanilla extract. Mix until well combined.
3. Gradually pour the wet ingredients into the dry ingredients, stirring until just combined. Be careful not to overmix; the batter should be slightly lumpy.
4. Lightly grease the air fryer basket with butter or cooking oil spray.
5. Spoon the pancake batter into the air fryer basket, forming pancakes of your desired size. Leave some space between each pancake for even cooking.
6. Evenly dividing them in between the two zone of the air fryer. Select Zone 1, choose the BAKE program, and set temperature to 180°C. Set time to 4-5 minutes. Select MATCH. Press the START/STOP.
7. After 2-3 minutes, carefully flip the pancakes using a spatula to ensure even cooking.
8. Continue cooking for another 2-3 minutes or until the **pancakes** are golden brown.
9. Once cooked, remove the pancakes from the air fryer and serve them warm.

# Breakfast Bruschetta

🕐 **Cooking Time: 12** Min  🍴 **Servings: 4 breakfast bruschetta**

- 4 slices of bread (baguette or ciabatta)
- 2 tbsp olive oil
- 4 large eggs
- Salt and pepper to taste
- 1 avocado, sliced
- 1 tomato, diced
- 2 tbsp chopped fresh basil
- Optional toppings: shredded cheese, cooked bacon or ham, hot sauce

# Morning Quiche

🕐 **Cooking Time: 6** Min  🍴 **Servings: 12 pancake bites**

- 4 large eggs
- 4 slices of bacon, cooked and crumbled
- 1/2 small onion, finely chopped
- 1/2 red bell pepper, diced
- 50g cheddar cheese, grated
- 50ml milk
- Salt and pepper to taste
- Cooking oil spray.

---

## INSTRUCTION

1. Brush both sides of the bread slices with olive oil.
2. Place the bread slices in Zone 1 of the air fryer basket, ensuring they are not too close together.
3. Select Zone 1, choose the AIR FRY program, and set the temperature to 180°C. Set the time to 3-4 minutes.
4. Press the START/STOP button to begin toasting the bread slices.
5. While the bread is toasting, crack an egg into each compartment of the air fryer basket. Season with salt and pepper to taste.
6. Place the basket in Zone 2 of the air fryer. Select Zone 2, choose the AIR FRY program, and set the temperature to 180°C. Set the time to 5-6 minutes for sunny-side-up eggs or 7-8 minutes for over-easy eggs.
7. Press the START/STOP button to begin cooking the eggs.
8. Once the bread is toasted and the eggs are cooked to your liking, remove them from the air fryer.
9. Top each toasted bread slice with sliced avocado, diced tomato, and a cooked egg.
10. Sprinkle chopped fresh basil over the top.
11. Add any optional toppings such as shredded cheese, cooked bacon or ham, or hot sauce, if desired.
12. Serve the **breakfast bruschetta** immediately for a delicious and satisfying breakfast.

---

1. Spray Zone 1 with cooking oil spray.
2. In a bowl, beat the eggs and milk together. Season with salt and pepper.
3. In another bowl, combine the cooked bacon, chopped onion, and diced red bell pepper.
4. Divide the bacon and vegetable mixture evenly into two individual ramekins.
5. Pour the egg mixture over the bacon and vegetables in each ramekin. Top with grated cheddar cheese.
6. Place the ramekins in Zone 1 of the air fryer. Make sure they are stable and won't tip over.
7. Select Zone 1, choose the AIR FRY program, and set the temperature to 180°C. Set the time to 15 minutes (or until the eggs are set and the cheese is melted and golden brown).
8. Once cooked, carefully remove the quiches from the air fryer using oven mitts or tongs.
9. Allow the quiches to cool for a few minutes before serving.
10. Serve the **Breakfast Quiche** warm as a delicious and filling breakfast. The combination of bacon, vegetables, and cheese creates a flavorful and satisfying dish. Enjoy!

## Fish & Chips

🕐 **Cooking Time: 15 Min**   🍴 **Servings: 2**

- 2 cod fillets (about 200g each)
- 60g all-purpose flour
- 1 large egg, beaten
- 60g breadcrumbs
- Salt and pepper to taste
- Cooking oil spray
- 4 large potatoes, peeled and cut into thick strips
- 1-2 tbsp olive oil

## Chicken Nuggets

🕐 **Cooking Time: 15 Min**   🍴 **Servings: 4**

- 400g boneless, skinless chicken breasts, cut into bite-sized pieces
- 60g all-purpose flour
- 2 large eggs, beaten
- 100g breadcrumbs
- 1/2 tsp paprika
- 1/2 tsp garlic powder
- 1/2 tsp onion powder
- Salt and pepper to taste
- Cooking oil spray

---

## INSTRUCTION

1. Prepare the fish: Pat the cod fillets dry with paper towels. Season with salt and pepper.
2. Set up a breading station: Place the flour on a plate, the beaten egg in a shallow bowl, and the breadcrumbs on another plate.
3. Dredge each cod fillet in the flour, shaking off any excess. Dip the fillets into the beaten egg, allowing any excess to drip off. Finally, coat the fillets in the breadcrumbs, pressing gently to adhere.
4. Lightly grease Zone 1 of the air fryer basket with cooking oil spray. Place the breaded fish fillets in Zone 1, ensuring they are not too crowded.
5. Prepare the chips: In a bowl, toss the potato strips with olive oil and salt until evenly coated.
6. Place the potato strips in Zone 2 of the air fryer basket.
7. Select Zone 1, choose the AIR FRY program, and set the temperature to 200°C. Set the time to 10-12 minutes. Select MATCH. Press the START/STOP button to begin cooking.
8. After 5-6 minutes, carefully flip the fish fillets and toss the potato strips to ensure even cooking.
9. Continue cooking for another 5-6 minutes or until the fish is golden brown and the chips are crispy.
10. Once cooked, remove the fish and chips from the air fryer.
11. Serve the **fish and chips** hot with tartar sauce, malt vinegar, or your preferred condiments.

---

1. In a shallow bowl, mix the breadcrumbs with paprika, garlic powder, onion powder, salt, and pepper.
2. Set up a breading station: Place the flour in one bowl, the beaten eggs in another bowl, and the seasoned breadcrumbs in a third bowl.
3. Dredge each chicken piece in the flour, shaking off any excess. Dip the floured chicken into the beaten eggs, allowing any excess to drip off. Finally, coat the chicken in the seasoned breadcrumbs, pressing gently to adhere.
4. Lightly grease Zone 1 of the air fryer basket with cooking oil spray. Place the breaded chicken nuggets in Zone 1, ensuring they are not too crowded.
5. Select Zone 1, choose the AIR FRY program, and set the temperature to 200°C. Set the time to 10-12 minutes. Press the START/STOP button to begin cooking.
6. After 5-6 minutes, carefully flip the chicken nuggets using tongs to ensure even cooking.
7. Continue cooking for another 5-6 minutes or until the chicken nuggets are golden brown and cooked through.
8. Once cooked, remove the chicken nuggets from the air fryer and let them cool slightly before serving.
9. Serve the **chicken nuggets** with your favorite dipping sauce

## Cheese & Onion Pasties

⏱ **Cooking Time:** 20 Min  🍴 **Servings:** 4 pasties

- 1 sheet ready-rolled shortcrust pastry (about 320g)
- 1 large onion, finely chopped
- 150g grated Cheddar cheese
- 1 tbsp butter
- 1 tbsp all-purpose flour
- Salt and pepper to taste
- 1 egg, beaten (for egg wash)

## Chicken Drumsticks

⏱ **Cooking Time:** 30 Min   **Servings:** 4

- 8 chicken drumsticks
- 2 tbsp olive oil
- 2 tsp smoked paprika
- 1 tsp garlic powder
- 1 tsp onion powder
- 1 tsp dried thyme
- 1 tsp salt
- 1/2 tsp black pepper

---

## INSTRUCTION

---

1. Cook the finely chopped onion in butter until soft, then stir in the flour and cook for 1-2 minutes.
2. Remove from heat, stir in the grated Cheddar cheese, and season with salt and pepper.
3. Roll out the shortcrust pastry and cut into 4 squares.
4. Divide the cheese and onion mixture among the squares, fold them into triangles, and crimp the edges with a fork.
5. Lightly grease Zone 1 of the air fryer basket with cooking oil spray.
6. Place the pasties in Zone 1, ensuring they are not too crowded.
7. Select Zone 1, choose the AIR FRY program, and set the temperature to 180°C. Set the time to 15-20 minutes.
8. Press the START/STOP button to begin cooking.
9. After 8-10 minutes, carefully flip the pasties using tongs.
10. Continue cooking for another 8-10 minutes or until golden brown and cooked through.
11. Remove the **pasties** from the air fryer and let them cool slightly before serving.

1. In a bowl, mix together the olive oil, smoked paprika, garlic powder, onion powder, dried thyme, salt, and black pepper to create a marinade.
2. Pat the chicken drumsticks dry with paper towels, then rub the marinade all over them, ensuring they are evenly coated.
3. Lightly grease Zone 1 of the air fryer basket with cooking oil spray. Place the chicken drumsticks in Zone 1, ensuring they are not too crowded.
4. Select Zone 1, choose the AIR FRY program, and set the temperature to 180°C. Set the time to 25-30 minutes.
5. Press the START/STOP button to begin cooking.
6. After 15 minutes, carefully flip the chicken drumsticks using tongs to ensure even cooking.
7. Continue cooking for another 10-15 minutes or until the chicken is golden brown and cooked through (internal temperature of 75°C).
8. Once cooked, remove the chicken drumsticks from the air fryer and let them rest for a few minutes before serving.
9. Serve the **chicken drumsticks** hot with your favorite sides.

## Vegetable Spring Rolls

🕐 **Cooking Time:** 12 Min  🍽 **Servings:** 12 spring rolls

- 200g bean sprouts
- 100g carrots, julienned
- 100g cabbage, shredded
- 50g spring onions, chopped
- 1 tbsp soy sauce
- 1 tsp sesame oil
- 1/2 tsp ground black pepper
- 12 spring roll wrappers
- Cooking oil spray

## Scotch Eggs

🕐 **Cooking Time:** 20 Min  🍽 **Servings:** 6 Scotch eggs

- 6 large eggs
- 500g sausage meat
- 100g breadcrumbs
- 1 tsp dried parsley
- 1/2 tsp dried thyme
- 1/2 tsp dried sage
- Salt and pepper to taste
- Cooking oil spray

## INSTRUCTION

1. In a bowl, mix together the bean sprouts, carrots, cabbage, spring onions, soy sauce, sesame oil, and black pepper.
2. Place a spring roll wrapper on a clean surface with one corner pointing towards you. Spoon some of the vegetable mixture onto the bottom third of the wrapper.
3. Fold the bottom corner of the wrapper over the filling, tuck in the sides, and roll up tightly.
4. Lightly grease both Zone of the air fryer basket with cooking oil spray. Evenly dividing rolls in between the two zone of the air fryer
5. Select Zone 1, choose the AIR FRY program, and set the temperature to 180°C. Set the time to 10-12 minutes. Select MATCH. Press the START/STOP button to begin cooking.
6. After 5-6 minutes, carefully flip the spring rolls using tongs to ensure even cooking.
7. Continue cooking for another 5-6 minutes or until the spring rolls are golden brown and crispy.
8. Once cooked, remove the **spring rolls** from the air fryer and let them cool slightly before serving.

1. Place the eggs in a saucepan and cover them with cold water. Bring the water to a boil, then reduce the heat and simmer for 6-7 minutes for a slightly soft yolk or 9-10 minutes for a firm yolk.
2. Once cooked, remove the eggs from the saucepan and place them in a bowl of cold water to stop the cooking process. Peel the eggs and set them aside.
3. In a bowl, mix together the sausage meat, breadcrumbs, dried parsley, dried thyme, dried sage, salt, and pepper until well combined.
4. Divide the sausage mixture into 6 equal portions. Flatten each portion into a disc shape.
5. Place a peeled egg in the center of each sausage disc, then wrap the sausage meat around the egg, ensuring it is fully covered.
6. Lightly grease Zone 1 of the air fryer basket with cooking oil spray. Place the Scotch eggs in Zone 1, ensuring they are not too crowded.
7. Select Zone 1, choose the AIR FRY program, and set the temperature to 180°C. Set the time to 15-20 minutes. Press the START/STOP.
8. After 8-10 minutes, carefully flip the Scotch eggs using tongs to ensure even cooking.
9. Continue cooking for another 8-10 minutes or until the Scotch eggs are golden brown and cooked through.
10. Once cooked, remove the **Scotch eggs** from the air fryer and let them cool slightly before serving.

# Homemade Chicken Burgers

⏱ **Cooking Time: 20 Min**  🍴 **Servings: 4 burgers**

- 500g ground chicken
- 1 small onion, finely chopped
- 2 garlic cloves, minced
- 1 tbsp fresh parsley, chopped
- 1 tbsp fresh cilantro, chopped
- 1 tsp paprika
- 1/2 tsp cumin
- 1/2 tsp salt
- 1/4 tsp black pepper
- 1 egg, beaten
- 4 burger buns
- Lettuce leaves, tomato slices, and other desired toppings
- Cooking oil spray

# Beef & Vegetable Pies

⏱ **Cooking Time: 20 Min**  🍴 **Servings: 4 individual pies**

- 500g beef mince
- 1 onion, finely chopped
- 2 carrots, diced
- 1 celery stalk, diced
- 1 tbsp tomato paste
- 1 tbsp Worcestershire sauce
- 120g beef stock
- Salt and pepper to taste
- 2 sheets ready-rolled puff pastry
- 1 egg, beaten (for egg wash)
- Cooking oil spray

## INSTRUCTION

1. In a large bowl, mix together the ground chicken, chopped onion, minced garlic, chopped parsley, chopped cilantro, paprika, cumin, salt, black pepper, and beaten egg until well combined.
2. Divide the mixture into 4 equal portions and shape them into burger patties.
3. Lightly grease Zone 1 of the air fryer basket with cooking oil spray. Place the burger patties in Zone 1, ensuring they are not too crowded.
4. Select Zone 1, choose the AIR FRY program, and set the temperature to 180°C. Set the time to 15-20 minutes.
5. Press the START/STOP button to begin cooking.
6. After 8-10 minutes, carefully flip the burger patties using a spatula to ensure even cooking.
7. Continue cooking for another 8-10 minutes or until the chicken burgers are cooked through and golden brown.
8. Once cooked, remove the chicken burgers from the air fryer and let them rest for a few minutes.
9. Toast the burger buns in the air fryer if desired.
10. Assemble the **burgers** by placing a chicken patty on each bun and topping with lettuce leaves, tomato slices, and any other desired toppings.

1. Cook beef mince, onion, carrots, and celery in a pan until beef is browned and vegetables are soft.
2. Add tomato paste, Worcestershire sauce, beef stock, salt, and pepper. Simmer until thickened. Let it cool slightly.
3. Line pie dishes with puff pastry. Divide beef mixture among the dishes.
4. Cover pies with remaining puff pastry. Seal edges and cut slits in the top.
5. Lightly grease Zone 1 of the air fryer basket with cooking oil spray. Place the pies in Zone 1, ensuring they are not too crowded.
6. Select Zone 1, choose the AIR FRY program, and set the temperature to 180°C. Set the time to 15-20 minutes.
7. Brush the tops of the pies with beaten egg.
8. Press the START/STOP button to begin cooking.
9. After 8-10 minutes, check the pies. Cover with foil if they're browning too quickly.
10. Continue cooking for another 8-10 minutes or until golden brown and cooked through.
11. Once cooked, remove the **pies** from the air fryer and let them cool slightly before serving.

## Stuffed Mushrooms

🕐 **Cooking Time:** 12  Min   🍴 **Servings:** 12 stuffed mushrooms

- 12 large mushrooms
- 120g cream cheese
- 30g grated Parmesan cheese
- 2 cloves garlic, minced
- 2 tbsp chopped fresh parsley
- Salt and pepper to taste
- Cooking oil spray

## Pork Chops

🕐 **Cooking Time:** 15  Min   🍴 **Servings:** 4

- 4 pork chops
- 2 tbsp olive oil
- 1 tsp paprika
- 1 tsp garlic powder
- 1 tsp onion powder
- 1/2 tsp dried thyme
- 1/2 tsp dried rosemary
- Salt and pepper to taste
- Cooking oil spray

## INSTRUCTION

1. Remove the stems from the mushrooms and finely chop them.
2. In a bowl, mix together the chopped mushroom stems, cream cheese, grated Parmesan cheese, minced garlic, chopped fresh parsley, salt, and pepper until well combined.
3. Spoon the cream cheese mixture into the mushroom caps, filling them evenly.
4. Lightly grease Zone 1 of the air fryer basket with cooking oil spray. Place the stuffed mushrooms in Zone 1, ensuring they are not too crowded.
5. Select Zone 1, choose the AIR FRY program, and set the temperature to 180°C. Set the time to 10-12 minutes.
6. Press the START/STOP button to begin cooking.
7. After 5-6 minutes, carefully check the stuffed mushrooms. If they are browning too quickly, you can cover them with foil to prevent over-browning.
8. Continue cooking for another 5-6 minutes or until the mushrooms are tender and the filling is golden brown and bubbly.
9. Once cooked, remove the **stuffed mushrooms** from the air fryer and let them cool slightly before serving.

---

1. In a small bowl, mix together the olive oil, paprika, garlic powder, onion powder, dried thyme, dried rosemary, salt, and pepper to form a paste.
2. Rub the paste over both sides of the pork chops, ensuring they are evenly coated.
3. Lightly grease Zone 1 of the air fryer basket with cooking oil spray. Place the pork chops in Zone 1, ensuring they are not too crowded.
4. Select Zone 1, choose the AIR FRY program, and set the temperature to 200°C. Set the time to 12-15 minutes.
5. Press the START/STOP button to begin cooking.
6. After 6-8 minutes, carefully flip the pork chops using tongs to ensure even cooking.
7. Continue cooking for another 6-8 minutes or until the pork chops reach an internal temperature of 63°C and are golden brown on the outside.
8. Once cooked, remove the **pork chops** from the air fryer and let them rest for a few minutes before serving.

# Breaded Mozzarella Sticks

🕐 Cooking Time: 8    Min    🍴 Servings: 12 mozzarella sticks

- 250g mozzarella cheese
- 60g all-purpose flour
- 2 eggs, beaten
- 100g breadcrumbs
- 1/2 tsp garlic powder
- 1/2 tsp dried oregano
- 1/2 tsp dried basil
- 1/4 tsp salt
- Cooking oil spray

# Potato Wedges

🕐 Cooking Time: 25   Min   🍴 Servings: 4

- 4 large potatoes
- 2 tbsp olive oil
- 1 tsp paprika
- 1/2 tsp garlic powder
- 1/2 tsp onion powder
- 1/2 tsp dried oregano
- 1/2 tsp dried thyme
- Salt and pepper to taste
- Cooking oil spray

## INSTRUCTION

1. Cut the mozzarella cheese into sticks, about 1.25 cm thick and 7.5 cm long.
2. In a shallow dish, mix together the breadcrumbs, garlic powder, dried oregano, dried basil, and salt.
3. Place the flour in another shallow dish and the beaten eggs in a third shallow dish.
4. Coat each mozzarella stick in the flour, then dip it into the beaten eggs, and finally coat it with the breadcrumb mixture, pressing gently to adhere.
5. Lightly grease Zone 1 of the air fryer basket with cooking oil spray. Place the breaded mozzarella sticks in Zone 1, ensuring they are not too crowded.
6. Select Zone 1, choose the AIR FRY program, and set the temperature to 200°C. Set the time to 6-8 minutes.
7. Press the START/STOP button to begin cooking.
8. After 3-4 minutes, carefully flip the mozzarella sticks using tongs to ensure even cooking.
9. Continue cooking for another 3-4 minutes or until the mozzarella sticks are golden brown and crispy.
10. Once cooked, remove the **mozzarella sticks** from the air fryer and let them cool slightly before serving.

1. Wash the potatoes and cut them into wedges.
2. In a large bowl, toss the potato wedges with olive oil, paprika, garlic powder, onion powder, dried oregano, dried thyme, salt, and pepper until evenly coated.
3. Lightly grease Zone 1 of the air fryer basket with cooking oil spray. Place the potato wedges in Zone 1, ensuring they are not too crowded.
4. Select Zone 1, choose the AIR FRY program, and set the temperature to 200°C. Set the time to 20-25 minutes.
5. Press the START/STOP button to begin cooking.
6. After 10-12 minutes, carefully shake or turn the potato wedges using tongs to ensure even cooking.
7. Continue cooking for another 10-12 minutes or until the potato wedges are crispy and golden brown.
8. Once cooked, remove the **potato wedges** from the air fryer and let them cool slightly before serving.

# Vegetable Samosas

⏱ **Cooking Time: 15 Min**  🍴 **Servings: 12 samosas**

- 2 large potatoes, boiled and mashed
- 160 g mixed vegetables (peas, carrots, corn), cooked
- 1 onion, finely chopped
- 2 green chilies, finely chopped
- 1 tsp ginger-garlic paste
- 1/2 tsp cumin seeds
- 1/2 tsp garam masala
- 1/2 tsp ground coriander
- 1/2 tsp ground cumin
- 1/2 tsp turmeric powder
- 12 samosa pastry sheets
- Salt to taste
- 2 tbsp chopped fresh coriander leaves
- Cooking oil spray

# Air-Fried Lasagna Rolls

⏱ **Cooking Time: 15 Min**  🍴 **Servings: 8 lasagna rolls**

- 8 lasagna noodles
- 250g ricotta cheese
- 100g shredded mozzarella cheese
- 25g grated Parmesan cheese
- 1 egg
- 1/2 teaspoon dried basil
- 1/2 teaspoon dried oregano
- 1/4 teaspoon garlic powder
- Salt and pepper to taste
- 500ml marinara sauce
- Cooking oil spray

## INSTRUCTION

1. In a pan, heat a little oil and add cumin seeds. When the seeds crackle, add the chopped onions and green chilies. Sauté until the onions are translucent.
2. Add ginger-garlic paste and sauté for a minute. Then, add the mashed potatoes and cooked mixed vegetables.
3. Add garam masala, ground coriander, ground cumin, turmeric powder, and salt. Mix well and cook for a few minutes. Remove from heat and let the mixture cool.
4. Take one samosa pastry sheet and fold it into a cone shape, sealing the edges with a little water.
5. Fill the cone with the cooled vegetable mixture and seal the open end using a little water to make a triangular samosa shape.
6. Lightly grease Zone 1 of the air fryer basket with cooking oil spray. Place the samosas in Zone 1, ensuring they are not too crowded.
7. Select Zone 1, choose the AIR FRY program, and set the temperature to 180°C. Set the time to 10-12 minutes. Press the START/STOP.
8. After 5-6 minutes, carefully flip the samosas using tongs to ensure even cooking.
9. Continue cooking for another 5-6 minutes or until the samosas are golden brown and crispy.
10. Once cooked, remove the **samosas** from the air fryer and let them cool slightly before serving.

1. Cook the lasagna noodles according to the package instructions. Drain and set aside to cool.
2. In a mixing bowl, combine the ricotta cheese, mozzarella cheese, Parmesan cheese, egg, basil, oregano, garlic powder, salt, and pepper. Mix well.
3. Lay out a lasagna noodle on a flat surface and spread a thin layer of the cheese mixture over the noodle.
4. Carefully roll up the noodle and place it seam-side down in the air fryer basket.
5. Repeat with the remaining noodles and cheese mixture, arranging the rolls in a single layer in Zone 1 of the air fryer basket, ensuring they are not too crowded.
6. Lightly grease Zone 1 of the air fryer basket with cooking oil spray.
7. Select Zone 1, choose the AIR FRY program, and set the temperature to 180°C. Set the time to 10-12 minutes. Press the START/STOP.
8. After 5-6 minutes, carefully flip the lasagna rolls using tongs to ensure even cooking.
9. Continue cooking for another 5-6 minutes or until the lasagna rolls are golden brown and heated through.
10. Once cooked, remove the lasagna rolls from the air fryer and let them cool slightly before serving. Serve the **lasagna rolls** with marinara sauce for dipping.

# Mushroom Risotto Balls

🕐 **Cooking Time:** 15 Min  🍴 **Servings:** 20 risotto balls

- 200g Arborio rice
- 750ml vegetable stock
- 1 onion, finely chopped
- 200g mushrooms, finely chopped
- 50g grated Parmesan cheese
- 2 eggs, beaten
- 100g breadcrumbs
- 2 tbsp chopped fresh parsley
- Salt and pepper to taste
- Cooking oil spray

# Beef & Onion Sausages

🕐 **Cooking Time:** 15 Min  🍴 **Servings:** 6 sausages

- 500g ground beef
- 1 small onion, finely chopped
- 1 garlic clove, minced
- 1 tsp dried thyme
- 1 tsp dried rosemary
- 1/2 tsp salt
- 1/4 tsp black pepper
- Cooking oil spray

## INSTRUCTION

1. Simmer the vegetable stock in a saucepan over low heat.
2. In a separate pan, sauté the onions until translucent, then add the Arborio rice and cook for 1-2 minutes.
3. Gradually add the warm vegetable stock to the rice, stirring constantly until absorbed and the rice is creamy and al dente.
4. Stir in the chopped mushrooms, cook for 5 more minutes, then remove from heat.
5. Mix in the Parmesan cheese, parsley, salt, and pepper. Let the mixture cool slightly, then shape it into small balls.
6. Dip each ball into beaten eggs, then roll in breadcrumbs until coated.
7. Lightly grease Zone 1 of the air fryer basket with cooking oil spray. Place the risotto balls in Zone 1.
8. Select Zone 1, choose the AIR FRY program, set the temperature to 180°C, and cook for 12-15 minutes, press the START/STOP button to begin cooking, flipping halfway through.
9. Once golden brown and crispy, remove the **risotto balls** from the air fryer and let them cool slightly before serving.

1. In a mixing bowl, combine the ground beef, chopped onion, minced garlic, dried thyme, dried rosemary, salt, and black pepper. Mix until well combined.
2. Divide the mixture into equal portions and shape each portion into a sausage shape.
3. Lightly grease Zone 1 of the air fryer basket with cooking oil spray. Place the sausages in Zone 1, ensuring they are not too crowded.
4. Select Zone 1, choose the AIR FRY program, and set the temperature to 180°C. Set the time to 12-15 minutes.
5. Press the START/STOP button to begin cooking.
6. After 6-8 minutes, carefully flip the sausages using tongs to ensure even cooking.
7. Continue cooking for another 6-8 minutes or until the sausages are browned and cooked through.
8. Once cooked, remove the **sausages** from the air fryer and let them cool slightly before serving.

## Crispy Chicken Tenders

🕐 **Cooking Time: 15　Min**　🍴 **Servings: 4**

- 500g chicken breast, cut into strips
- 100 g breadcrumbs
- 50 g grated Parmesan cheese
- 1 tsp paprika
- 1 tsp garlic powder
- 1/2 tsp salt
- 1/4 tsp black pepper
- 2 eggs, beaten
- Cooking oil spray

## Cheesy Garlic Breadsticks

🕐 **Cooking Time: 10　Min**　🍴 **Servings: 12 breadsticks**

- 1 tube (11 oz or approximately 312g) refrigerated breadstick dough
- 60g unsalted butter, melted
- 2 cloves garlic, minced
- 25g grated Parmesan cheese
- 60g shredded mozzarella cheese
- 2.5ml dried oregano
- 2.5ml dried basil
- Cooking oil spray

## INSTRUCTION

1. In a bowl, mix together the breadcrumbs, grated Parmesan cheese, paprika, garlic powder, salt, and black pepper.
2. Dip each chicken strip into the beaten eggs, then coat it with the breadcrumb mixture, pressing gently to adhere.
3. Lightly grease Zone 1 of the air fryer basket with cooking oil spray. Place the coated chicken tenders in Zone 1, ensuring they are not too crowded.
4. Select Zone 1, choose the AIR FRY program, and set the temperature to 180°C. Set the time to 12-15 minutes.
5. Press the START/STOP button to begin cooking.
6. After 6-8 minutes, carefully flip the chicken tenders using tongs to ensure even cooking.
7. Continue cooking for another 6-8 minutes or until the chicken tenders are golden brown and crispy.
8. Once cooked, remove the **chicken tenders** from the air fryer and let them cool slightly before serving.

1. Open the tube of refrigerated breadstick dough and separate the individual breadsticks.
2. In a small bowl, mix the melted butter and minced garlic together.
3. Dip each breadstick into the garlic butter mixture, then twist them and place them in Zone 1 of the air fryer basket.
4. Sprinkle the breadsticks with grated Parmesan cheese, shredded mozzarella cheese, dried oregano, and dried basil.
5. Lightly grease Zone 1 of the air fryer basket with cooking oil spray.
6. Select Zone 1, choose the AIR FRY program, and set the temperature to 180°C. Set the time to 8-10 minutes.
7. Press the START/STOP button to begin cooking.
8. After 4-5 minutes, carefully flip the breadsticks using tongs to ensure even cooking.
9. Continue cooking for another 4-5 minutes or until the breadsticks are golden brown and the cheese is melted and bubbly.
10. Once cooked, remove the **breadsticks** from the air fryer and let them cool slightly before serving.

## Prawn Spring Rolls

🕐 **Cooking Time:** 12 Min  🍴 **Servings:** 12 spring rolls

- 200g cooked prawns, chopped
- 100g shredded cabbage
- 50g shredded carrots
- 50g bean sprouts
- 2 spring onions, finely chopped
- 1 garlic clove, minced
- 1 tsp grated ginger
- 1 tbsp soy sauce
- 1 tsp fish sauce
- 1 tsp sesame oil
- 12 spring roll wrappers
- Cooking oil spray

## Chicken Quesadillas

🕐 **Cooking Time:** 10 Min  🍴 **Servings:** 2 quesadillas

- 2 large flour tortillas
- 200g cooked chicken breast, shredded
- 100g shredded cheddar cheese
- 50g diced tomatoes
- 50g diced green bell pepper
- 1/2 teaspoon ground cumin
- 1/2 teaspoon chili powder
- 1/2 teaspoon garlic powder
- Salt and pepper to taste
- Cooking oil spray

## INSTRUCTION

1. In a bowl, combine the chopped prawns, shredded cabbage, shredded carrots, bean sprouts, chopped spring onions, minced garlic, grated ginger, soy sauce, fish sauce, and sesame oil. Mix well to combine.
2. Place a spring roll wrapper on a clean surface. Spoon about 2 tablespoons of the prawn mixture onto the bottom third of the wrapper.
3. Fold the bottom of the wrapper over the filling, then fold in the sides, and roll it up tightly.
4. Lightly grease both Zone of the air fryer basket with cooking oil spray. Evenly dividing rolls between the two zone, ensuring they are not too crowded.
5. Select Zone 1, choose the AIR FRY program, and set the temperature to 180°C. Set the time to 10-12 minutes. Select MATCH to duplicate settings across both zones.
6. Press the START/STOP to begin cooking.
7. After 5-6 minutes, carefully flip the spring rolls using tongs to ensure even cooking.
8. Continue cooking for another 5-6 minutes or until the spring rolls are golden brown and crispy.
9. Once cooked, remove the **spring rolls** from the air fryer and let them cool slightly before serving.

---

1. In a bowl, mix the shredded chicken with the diced tomatoes, diced green bell pepper, ground cumin, chili powder, garlic powder, salt, and pepper.
2. Place one flour tortilla on a flat surface. Spread half of the chicken mixture evenly over one half of the tortilla, leaving a small border around the edge.
3. Sprinkle half of the shredded cheddar cheese over the chicken mixture.
4. Fold the tortilla in half to cover the filling, pressing down gently to seal.
5. Lightly grease both Zone of the air fryer basket with cooking oil spray. Place one quesadilla in each Zone.
6. Select Zone 1, choose the AIR FRY program, and set the temperature to 180°C. Set the time to 5-6 minutes. Select MATCH to duplicate settings across both zones.
7. After 2-3 minutes, carefully flip the quesadilla using tongs to ensure even cooking.
8. Continue cooking for another 2-3 minutes or until the quesadilla is golden brown and the cheese is melted.
9. Once cooked, remove the **quesadilla** from the air fryer and let it cool slightly before cutting into wedges.

# Macaroni & Cheese Bites

**Cooking Time:** 12 Min  **Servings:** 20 macaroni & cheese bites

- 200g elbow macaroni
- 200g shredded cheddar cheese
- 50g grated Parmesan cheese
- 1 egg, beaten
- 50g plain flour
- 50g breadcrumbs
- 1/2 teaspoon garlic powder
- 1/2 teaspoon onion powder
- Salt and pepper to taste
- Cooking oil spray

# Homemade Fish Fingers

**Cooking Time:** 15 Min  **Servings:** 4

- 400g white fish fillets (such as cod or haddock), cut into fingers
- 50g plain flour
- 2 eggs, beaten
- 100g breadcrumbs
- 1/2 teaspoon paprika
- 1/2 teaspoon garlic powder
- 1/2 teaspoon onion powder
- Salt and pepper to taste
- Cooking oil spray

## INSTRUCTION

1. Cook the elbow macaroni according to the package instructions. Drain and set aside to cool slightly.
2. In a large bowl, combine the cooked macaroni, shredded cheddar cheese, grated Parmesan cheese, beaten egg, garlic powder, onion powder, salt, and pepper. Mix until well combined.
3. Using your hands, shape the macaroni mixture into bite-sized balls.
4. Place the plain flour, beaten egg, and breadcrumbs into separate shallow bowls.
5. Dip each macaroni ball into the plain flour, then the beaten egg, and finally the breadcrumbs, ensuring they are evenly coated.
6. Lightly grease Zone 1 of the air fryer basket with cooking oil spray. Place the coated macaroni balls in Zone 1.
7. Select Zone 1, choose the AIR FRY program, and set the temperature to 180°C. Set the time to 8-10 minutes.
8. Press the START/STOP button to begin cooking.
9. After 4-5 minutes, carefully flip the macaroni balls using tongs to ensure even cooking.
10. Continue cooking for another 4-5 minutes or until the **macaroni balls** are golden brown and crispy.
11. Once cooked, remove the macaroni balls from the air fryer and let them cool slightly before serving.

1. In a shallow bowl, mix together the breadcrumbs, paprika, garlic powder, onion powder, salt, and pepper.
2. Place the plain flour in another shallow bowl, and the beaten eggs in a third shallow bowl.
3. Dip each fish finger into the plain flour, then into the beaten egg, and finally into the breadcrumb mixture, pressing gently to coat evenly.
4. Lightly grease Zone 1 of the air fryer basket with cooking oil spray. Place the coated fish fingers in Zone 1, ensuring they are not too crowded.
5. Select Zone 1, choose the AIR FRY program, and set the temperature to 180°C. Set the time to 10-12 minutes.
6. Press the START/STOP button to begin cooking.
7. After 5-6 minutes, carefully flip the fish fingers using tongs to ensure even cooking.
8. Continue cooking for another 5-6 minutes or until the fish fingers are golden brown and cooked through.
9. Once cooked, remove the **fish fingers** from the air fryer and let them cool slightly before serving.

# Vegetarian Quesadillas

⏱ **Cooking Time:** 10 Min   **Servings:** 2 quesadillas

- 2 large flour tortillas
- 100g shredded mozzarella cheese
- 100g canned black beans, drained and rinsed
- 50g diced tomatoes
- 50g diced red bell pepper
- 50g diced green bell pepper
- 2 tbsp chopped fresh cilantro
- 1/2 tsp ground cumin
- 1/2 tsp chili powder
- Salt and pepper to taste
- Cooking oil spray

# Sweet Potato Fries

⏱ **Cooking Time:** 15 Min  **Servings:** 4

- 2 medium sweet potatoes, peeled and cut into thin strips
- 1-2 tablespoons olive oil
- 1/2 teaspoon paprika
- 1/2 teaspoon garlic powder
- 1/2 teaspoon onion powder
- Salt and pepper to taste
- Cooking oil spray

## INSTRUCTION

1. In a bowl, mix together the black beans, diced tomatoes, diced red bell pepper, diced green bell pepper, chopped fresh cilantro, ground cumin, chili powder, salt, and pepper.
2. Place one flour tortilla on a flat surface. Spread half of the shredded mozzarella cheese evenly over the tortilla.
3. Spoon half of the black bean mixture over the cheese, spreading it evenly.
4. Top with the second tortilla to cover the filling, pressing down gently.
5. Lightly grease both Zone of the air fryer basket with cooking oil spray. Place one quesadilla in each Zone.
6. Select Zone 1, choose the AIR FRY program, and set the temperature to 180°C. Set the time to 5-6 minutes. Select MATCH to duplicate settings across both zones. Press the START/STOP.
7. After 2-3 minutes, carefully flip the quesadilla using tongs to ensure even cooking.
8. Continue cooking for another 2-3 minutes or until the quesadilla is golden brown and the cheese is melted.
9. Once cooked, remove the **quesadilla** from the air fryer and let it cool slightly before cutting into wedges.

1. In a large bowl, toss the sweet potato strips with olive oil, paprika, garlic powder, onion powder, salt, and pepper until evenly coated.
2. Lightly grease Zone 1 of the air fryer basket with cooking oil spray. Place the sweet potato strips in Zone 1, ensuring they are in a single layer and not too crowded.
3. Select Zone 1, choose the AIR FRY program, and set the temperature to 200°C. Set the time to 12-15 minutes.
4. Press the START/STOP button to begin cooking.
5. After 6-8 minutes, carefully shake the basket or use tongs to flip the sweet potato strips for even cooking.
6. Continue cooking for another 6-8 minutes or until the sweet potato fries are crispy and golden brown.
7. Once cooked, remove the **sweet potato fries** from the air fryer and let them cool slightly before serving

# Quick Fish Fillets

🕐 **Cooking Time:** 10 Min   🍽 **Servings:** 4

- 4 fish fillets (such as cod, haddock, or tilapia)
- 2 tablespoons olive oil
- 1 teaspoon paprika
- 1/2 teaspoon garlic powder
- 1/2 teaspoon onion powder
- Salt and pepper to taste
- Lemon wedges, for serving
- Cooking oil spray

# Crispy Chicken Wings

🕐 **Cooking Time:** 30 Min   🍽 **Servings:** 4

- 1 kg chicken wings, split at the joints and tips discarded
- 2 tablespoons baking powder
- 1 teaspoon garlic powder
- 1 teaspoon onion powder
- 1 teaspoon paprika
- 1/2 teaspoon salt
- 1/2 teaspoon black pepper
- Cooking oil spray

---

## INSTRUCTION

---

1. In a small bowl, mix together the olive oil, paprika, garlic powder, onion powder, salt, and pepper.
2. Pat the fish fillets dry with paper towels and brush both sides of each fillet with the seasoned oil mixture.
3. Lightly grease Zone 1 of the air fryer basket with cooking oil spray. Place the fish fillets in Zone 1, ensuring they are not too crowded.
4. Select Zone 1, choose the AIR FRY program, and set the temperature to 200°C. Set the time to 8-10 minutes.
5. Press the START/STOP button to begin cooking.
6. After 4-5 minutes, carefully flip the fish fillets using tongs to ensure even cooking.
7. Continue cooking for another 4-5 minutes or until the fish is opaque and flakes easily with a fork.
8. Once cooked, remove the fish fillets from the air fryer and transfer them to a serving plate.
9. Serve the **fish fillets** with lemon wedges for squeezing over the top.

1. In a large bowl, mix together the baking powder, garlic powder, onion powder, paprika, salt, and black pepper.
2. Pat the chicken wings dry with paper towels, then add them to the bowl with the seasoning mixture. Toss the wings until they are evenly coated.
3. Lightly grease Zone 1 of the air fryer basket with cooking oil spray. Place the chicken wings in Zone 1, ensuring they are in a single layer and not too crowded.
4. Select Zone 1, choose the AIR FRY program, and set the temperature to 200°C. Set the time to 25-30 minutes.
5. Press the START/STOP button to begin cooking.
6. After 12-15 minutes, carefully flip the chicken wings using tongs to ensure even cooking.
7. Continue cooking for another 12-15 minutes or until the chicken wings are crispy and golden brown.
8. Once cooked, remove the **chicken wings** from the air fryer and let them cool slightly before serving.

# Cheese & Ham Quesadillas

Cooking Time: 12 Min   Servings: 2 quesadillas

- 2 large flour tortillas
- 100g shredded cheddar cheese
- 100g diced ham
- 50g diced tomatoes
- 50g diced red onion
- 2 tbsp chopped fresh cilantro
- Cooking oil spray

# Easy Vegetable Fritters

Cooking Time: 12 Min   Servings: 8 fritters

- 1 large zucchini, grated (about 200g)
- 1 large carrot, grated (about 200g)
- 75g frozen corn, thawed
- 65g plain flour
- 25g grated Parmesan cheese
- 2 eggs, beaten
- 2.5ml baking powder
- 2.5ml garlic powder
- 2.5ml onion powder
- Salt and pepper to taste
- Cooking oil spray

## INSTRUCTION

1. Place one flour tortilla on a flat surface. Sprinkle half of the shredded cheddar cheese evenly over the tortilla.
2. Spread half of the diced ham, diced tomatoes, diced red onion, and chopped fresh cilantro over the cheese.
3. Top with the second tortilla to cover the filling, pressing down gently.
4. Lightly grease both Zone of the air fryer basket with cooking oil spray. Place one quesadilla in each Zone.
5. Select Zone 1, choose the AIR FRY program, and set the temperature to 180°C. Set the time to 5-6 minutes. Select MATCH to duplicate settings across both zones. Press the START/STOP button to begin cooking.
6. After 2-3 minutes, carefully flip the quesadilla using tongs to ensure even cooking.
7. Continue cooking for another 2-3 minutes or until the quesadilla is golden brown and the cheese is melted.
8. Once cooked, remove the **quesadilla** from the air fryer and let it cool slightly before cutting into wedges.

1. In a large bowl, combine the grated zucchini, grated carrot, thawed corn, plain flour, grated Parmesan cheese, beaten eggs, baking powder, garlic powder, onion powder, salt, and pepper. Mix until well combined.
2. Lightly grease Zone 1 of the air fryer basket with cooking oil spray. Spoon the vegetable mixture into Zone 1, shaping it into fritters and ensuring they are not too crowded.
3. Select Zone 1, choose the AIR FRY program, and set the temperature to 200°C. Set the time to 10-12 minutes.
4. Press the START/STOP button to begin cooking.
5. After 5-6 minutes, carefully flip the vegetable fritters using tongs to ensure even cooking.
6. Continue cooking for another 5-6 minutes or until the fritters are golden brown and crispy.
7. Once cooked, remove the **vegetable fritters** from the air fryer and let them cool slightly before serving.

# Veggie Burgers

🕐 **Cooking Time:** 15 Min   🍴 **Servings:** 4-6 veggie burgers

- 400g canned chickpeas, drained and rinsed
- 200g cooked quinoa
- 100g grated carrot
- 1 small onion, finely chopped
- 2 cloves garlic, minced
- 50g breadcrumbs
- 1 egg, beaten
- 2 tbsp chopped fresh parsley
- 1 tsp ground cumin
- 1 tsp paprika
- Salt and pepper to taste
- Cooking oil spray

# Avocado Fries

🕐 **Cooking Time:** 10 Min   🍴 **Servings:** 4

- 2 ripe avocados
- 100g breadcrumbs
- 50g grated Parmesan cheese
- 1/2 tsp garlic powder
- 1/2 tsp paprika
- Salt and pepper to taste
- 2 eggs, beaten
- Cooking oil spray

## INSTRUCTION

1. In a large bowl, mash the chickpeas with a fork or potato masher until mostly smooth.
2. Add the cooked quinoa, grated carrot, chopped onion, minced garlic, breadcrumbs, beaten egg, chopped parsley, ground cumin, paprika, salt, and pepper to the mashed chickpeas. Mix until well combined.
3. Divide the mixture into equal portions and shape them into burger patties.
4. Lightly grease Zone 1 of the air fryer basket with cooking oil spray. Place the burger patties in Zone 1, ensuring they are not too crowded.
5. Select Zone 1, choose the AIR FRY program, and set the temperature to 200°C. Set the time to 12-15 minutes.
6. Press the START/STOP button to begin cooking.
7. After 6-8 minutes, carefully flip the burger patties using tongs to ensure even cooking.
8. Continue cooking for another 6-8 minutes or until the veggie burgers are golden brown and crispy.
9. Once cooked, remove the **veggie burgers** from the air fryer and assemble them in buns with your favorite toppings.

1. Cut the avocados in half lengthwise, remove the pits, and slice each half into wedges.
2. In a shallow bowl, mix together the breadcrumbs, grated Parmesan cheese, garlic powder, paprika, salt, and pepper.
3. Dip each avocado wedge into the beaten eggs, then coat them with the breadcrumb mixture, pressing gently to adhere.
4. Lightly grease both Zone of the air fryer baskets with cooking oil spray. Place the coated avocado wedges in both Zone, ensuring they are not too crowded.
5. Select Zone 1, choose the AIR FRY program, and set the temperature to 200°C. Set the time to 8-10 minutes.
6. Select MATCH to duplicate settings across both zones Press the START/STOP button to begin cooking.
7. After 4-5 minutes, carefully flip the avocado wedges using tongs to ensure even cooking.
8. Continue cooking for another 4-5 minutes or until the avocado fries are golden brown and crispy.
9. Once cooked, remove the **avocado fries** from the air fryer and let them cool slightly before serving.

# Zucchini Chips

⏱ **Cooking Time: 10 Min**  🍽 **Servings: 4**

- 2 medium zucchinis, thinly sliced
- 50g grated Parmesan cheese
- 50g breadcrumbs
- 1/2 tsp garlic powder
- 1/2 tsp paprika
- Salt and pepper to taste
- 2 eggs, beaten
- Cooking oil spray

# Veggie Sticks

⏱ **Cooking Time: 10 Min**  🍽 **Servings: 4**

- 2 large carrots
- 2 large zucchinis
- 1 large bell pepper (any color)
- 1 tbsp olive oil
- 1/2 tsp garlic powder
- 1/2 tsp paprika
- Salt and pepper to taste
- Cooking oil spray

## INSTRUCTION

1. In a shallow bowl, mix together the grated Parmesan cheese, breadcrumbs, garlic powder, paprika, salt, and pepper.
2. Dip each zucchini slice into the beaten eggs, then coat them with the breadcrumb mixture, pressing gently to adhere.
3. Lightly grease Zone 1 of the air fryer basket with cooking oil spray. Place the coated zucchini slices in Zone 1, ensuring they are not too crowded.
4. Select Zone 1, choose the AIR FRY program, and set the temperature to 200°C. Set the time to 8-10 minutes.
5. Press the START/STOP button to begin cooking.
6. After 4-5 minutes, carefully flip the zucchini slices using tongs to ensure even cooking.
7. Continue cooking for another 4-5 minutes or until the zucchini chips are golden brown and crispy.
8. Once cooked, remove the **zucchini chips** from the air fryer and let them cool slightly before serving.

1. Wash and peel the carrots. Cut the carrots, zucchinis, and bell pepper into stick shapes.
2. In a bowl, toss the veggie sticks with olive oil, garlic powder, paprika, salt, and pepper until well coated.
3. Lightly grease Zone 1 of the air fryer basket with cooking oil spray. Place the veggie sticks in Zone 1, ensuring they are in a single layer and not too crowded.
4. Select Zone 1, choose the AIR FRY program, and set the temperature to 200°C. Set the time to 8-10 minutes.
5. Press the START/STOP button to begin cooking.
6. After 4-5 minutes, carefully flip the veggie sticks using tongs to ensure even cooking.
7. Continue cooking for another 4-5 minutes or until the veggie sticks are tender and slightly crispy.
8. Once cooked, remove the **veggie sticks** from the air fryer and let them cool slightly before serving.

## Swift Garlic Bread

🕐 **Cooking Time:** 12 Min  🍽 **Servings:** 4-6

- 1 large baguette or loaf of bread
- 100g unsalted butter, softened
- 4 garlic cloves, minced
- 2 tbsp chopped fresh parsley
- Salt to taste

## Cheese Balls

🕐 **Cooking Time:** 10 Min  🍽 **Servings:** 20 cheese balls

- 200g shredded mozzarella cheese
- 100g grated Parmesan cheese
- 50g cream cheese
- 1 egg, beaten
- 50g breadcrumbs
- 1/2 tsp garlic powder
- 1/2 tsp onion powder
- 1/2 tsp dried oregano
- Salt and pepper to taste
- Cooking oil spray

---

## INSTRUCTION

---

1. In a bowl, mix together the softened butter, minced garlic, chopped fresh parsley, and salt until well combined.
2. Slice the baguette or loaf of bread into even slices, but do not cut all the way through so that the slices remain attached at the bottom.
3. Spread the garlic butter mixture between the slices, making sure to cover each slice evenly.
4. Wrap the bread loaf in foil, leaving the top exposed.
5. Lightly grease Zone 1 of the air fryer basket with cooking oil spray. Place the wrapped bread loaf in Zone 1.
6. Select Zone 1, choose the AIR FRY program, and set the temperature to 180°C. Set the time to 10-12 minutes.
7. Press the START/STOP button to begin cooking.
8. After 5-6 minutes, carefully open the foil to expose the top of the bread loaf.
9. Continue cooking for another 5-6 minutes or until the garlic bread is golden brown and crispy on top.
10. Once cooked, remove the **garlic bread** from the air fryer and let it cool slightly before serving.

1. In a bowl, mix together the shredded mozzarella cheese, grated Parmesan cheese, cream cheese, beaten egg, breadcrumbs, garlic powder, onion powder, dried oregano, salt, and pepper until well combined.
2. Shape the mixture into small balls, about 1 inch in diameter, and place them on a plate.
3. Lightly grease Zone 1 of the air fryer basket with cooking oil spray. Place the cheese balls in Zone 1, ensuring they are not too crowded.
4. Select Zone 1, choose the AIR FRY program, and set the temperature to 180°C. Set the time to 8-10 minutes.
5. Press the START/STOP button to begin cooking.
6. After 4-5 minutes, carefully flip the cheese balls using tongs to ensure even cooking.
7. Continue cooking for another 4-5 minutes or until the cheese balls are golden brown and crispy.
8. Once cooked, remove the **cheese balls** from the air fryer and let them cool slightly before serving.

# Sweetcorn Fritters

⏱ **Cooking Time:** 15 Min  🍴 **Servings:** 4-6 sweetcorn fritters

- 200g canned sweetcorn, drained
- 100g plain flour
- 1 egg, beaten
- 1/2 tsp baking powder
- 1/2 tsp paprika
- Salt and pepper to taste
- Cooking oil spray

# Quick Pita Chips

⏱ **Cooking Time:** 6 Min  🍴 **Servings:** 4-6

- 2 large pita breads
- 2 tbsp olive oil
- 1/2 tsp garlic powder
- 1/2 tsp paprika
- Salt to taste
- Cooking oil spray

---

## INSTRUCTION

1. In a bowl, combine the drained sweetcorn, plain flour, beaten egg, baking powder, paprika, salt, and pepper. Mix until well combined.
2. Lightly grease Zone 1 of the air fryer basket with cooking oil spray. Spoon the sweetcorn mixture into Zone 1, shaping it into fritters and ensuring they are not too crowded.
3. Select Zone 1, choose the AIR FRY program, and set the temperature to 180°C. Set the time to 10-12 minutes.
4. Press the START/STOP button to begin cooking.
5. After 5-6 minutes, carefully flip the sweetcorn fritters using tongs to ensure even cooking.
6. Continue cooking for another 5-6 minutes or until the fritters are golden brown and crispy.
7. Once cooked, remove the **sweetcorn fritters** from the air fryer and let them cool slightly before serving.

1. Cut the pita breads into wedges or squares.
2. In a bowl, mix together the olive oil, garlic powder, paprika, and salt.
3. Brush both sides of the pita bread pieces with the oil mixture.
4. Lightly grease Zone 1 of the air fryer basket with cooking oil spray. Place the pita bread pieces in Zone 1, ensuring they are in a single layer and not too crowded.
5. Select Zone 1, choose the AIR FRY program, and set the temperature to 180°C. Set the time to 4-6 minutes.
6. Press the START/STOP button to begin cooking.
7. After 2-3 minutes, carefully flip the pita bread pieces using tongs to ensure even cooking.
8. Continue cooking for another 2-3 minutes or until the pita chips are golden brown and crispy.
9. Once cooked, remove the **pita chips** from the air fryer and let them cool slightly before serving.

# Egg Rolls

🕐 **Cooking Time:** 15 Min   🍽 **Servings:** 8 egg rolls

- 8 egg roll wrappers
- 200g cooked and shredded chicken or pork
- 100g shredded cabbage
- 50g shredded carrots
- 50g sliced green onions
- 1 clove garlic, minced
- 1 tsp grated ginger
- 2 tbsp soy sauce
- 1 tbsp oyster sauce
- 1 tsp sesame oil
- 1/2 tsp sugar
- 1/2 tsp black pepper
- 1 egg, beaten (for sealing the egg rolls)
- Cooking oil spray

# Tofu Bites

🕐 **Cooking Time:** 12 Min   🍽 **Servings:** 4

- 400g firm tofu, drained and pressed
- 2 tbsp cornstarch
- 1 tbsp soy sauce
- 1 tbsp rice vinegar
- 1 tsp sesame oil
- 1/2 tsp garlic powder
- 1/2 tsp onion powder
- 1/4 tsp ground ginger
- Salt and pepper to taste
- Cooking oil spray

## INSTRUCTION

1. In a large bowl, combine the cooked and shredded chicken or pork, shredded cabbage, shredded carrots, sliced green onions, minced garlic, grated ginger, soy sauce, oyster sauce, sesame oil, sugar, and black pepper. Mix until well combined.
2. Lay an egg roll wrapper on a clean surface with one corner pointing towards you. Place about 2-3 tablespoons of the filling mixture in the center of the wrapper.
3. Fold the bottom corner over the filling, then fold in the sides, and roll up tightly. Brush the top corner with beaten egg to seal the egg roll.
4. Repeat with the remaining wrappers and filling.
5. Lightly grease both Zone of the air fryer basket with cooking oil spray.
6. Evenly dividing egg rolls between the two zone, ensuring they are in a single layer and not too crowded.
7. Select Zone 1, choose the AIR FRY program, and set the temperature to 180°C. Set the time to 10-12 minutes. Select MATCH to duplicate settings across both zones. Press the START/STOP.
8. After 5-6 minutes, carefully flip the egg rolls using tongs to ensure even cooking.
9. Continue cooking for another 5-6 minutes or until the egg rolls are golden brown and crispy.
10. Once cooked, remove the **egg rolls** from the air fryer and let them cool slightly before serving.

1. Cut the pressed tofu into bite-sized cubes.
2. In a bowl, mix together the cornstarch, soy sauce, rice vinegar, sesame oil, garlic powder, onion powder, ground ginger, salt, and pepper.
3. Add the tofu cubes to the bowl and gently toss to coat them evenly with the mixture.
4. Lightly grease Zone 1 of the air fryer basket with cooking oil spray. Place the coated tofu cubes in Zone 1, ensuring they are in a single layer and not too crowded.
5. Select Zone 1, choose the AIR FRY program, and set the temperature to 200°C. Set the time to 10-12 minutes.
6. Press the START/STOP button to begin cooking.
7. After 5-6 minutes, carefully shake the basket or flip the tofu cubes using tongs to ensure even cooking.
8. Continue cooking for another 5-6 minutes or until the tofu bites are golden brown and crispy.
9. Once cooked, remove the **tofu bites** from the air fryer and let them cool slightly before serving.

# Mediterranean Vegetables

⏱ **Cooking Time: 15 Min**   🍽 **Servings: 4**

- 2 bell peppers (any color), sliced
- 1 large zucchini, sliced
- 1 large red onion, sliced
- 200g cherry tomatoes
- 2 tbsp olive oil
- 2 cloves garlic, minced
- 1 tsp dried oregano
- 1 tsp dried basil
- Salt and pepper to taste
- Cooking oil spray

# Speedy Bacon

⏱ **Cooking Time: 10 Min**   🍽 **Servings: Depends on the number of bacon slices**

- Slices of bacon

## INSTRUCTION

1. In a large bowl, toss together the sliced bell peppers, zucchini, red onion, and cherry tomatoes with olive oil, minced garlic, dried oregano, dried basil, salt, and pepper until well coated.
2. Lightly grease Zone 1 of the air fryer basket with cooking oil spray. Place the seasoned vegetables in Zone 1, ensuring they are in a single layer and not too crowded.
3. Select Zone 1, choose the AIR FRY program, and set the temperature to 200°C. Set the time to 12-15 minutes.
4. Press the START/STOP button to begin cooking.
5. After 6-7 minutes, carefully shake the basket or stir the vegetables using tongs to ensure even cooking.
6. Continue cooking for another 6-7 minutes or until the vegetables are tender and slightly charred.
7. Once cooked, remove the **Mediterranean vegetables** from the air fryer and transfer them to a serving dish.

1. Arrange the bacon slices in a single layer in Zone 1 of the air fryer basket.
2. Select Zone 1, choose the AIR FRY program, and set the temperature to 180°C. Set the time to 8-10 minutes.
3. Press the START/STOP button to begin cooking.
4. After 4-5 minutes, carefully flip the bacon slices using tongs to ensure even cooking.
5. Continue cooking for another 4-5 minutes or until the bacon reaches your desired level of crispiness.
6. Once cooked, remove the **bacon** from the air fryer and place it on a plate lined with paper towels to absorb any excess grease.

# Rapid Shrimp

⏱ **Cooking Time:** 8  Min   🍴 **Servings:** 2-3

- 300g large shrimp, peeled and deveined
- 2 tbsp olive oil
- 2 cloves garlic, minced
- 1/2 tsp paprika
- 1/2 tsp dried oregano
- Salt and pepper to taste
- Lemon wedges for serving (optional)

# Garlic Parmesan Shrimp

⏱ **Cooking Time:** 10  Min   🍴 **Servings:** 2-3

- 300g large shrimp, peeled and deveined
- 2 tbsp melted butter
- 2 cloves garlic, minced
- 25 g grated Parmesan cheese
- 1/2 tsp paprika
- Salt and pepper to taste
- Lemon wedges for serving (optional)
- Chopped parsley for garnish (optional)

## INSTRUCTION

1. In a bowl, toss the shrimp with olive oil, minced garlic, paprika, dried oregano, salt, and pepper until evenly coated.
2. Lightly grease Zone 1 of the air fryer basket with cooking oil spray. Place the seasoned shrimp in Zone 1, ensuring they are in a single layer and not too crowded.
3. Select Zone 1, choose the AIR FRY program, and set the temperature to 200°C. Set the time to 6-8 minutes.
4. Press the START/STOP button to begin cooking.
5. After 3-4 minutes, carefully shake the basket or flip the shrimp using tongs to ensure even cooking.
6. Continue cooking for another 3-4 minutes or until the shrimp are pink and opaque.
7. Once cooked, remove the shrimp from the air fryer and transfer them to a serving plate.
8. Serve the **rapid shrimp** immediately with lemon wedges on the side, if desired.

---

1. In a bowl, combine the melted butter, minced garlic, grated Parmesan cheese, paprika, salt, and pepper.
2. Add the peeled and deveined shrimp to the bowl and toss until the shrimp are evenly coated with the mixture.
3. Lightly grease Zone 1 of the air fryer basket with cooking oil spray. Place the coated shrimp in Zone 1, ensuring they are in a single layer and not too crowded.
4. Select Zone 1, choose the AIR FRY program, and set the temperature to 200°C. Set the time to 6-8 minutes.
5. Press the START/STOP button to begin cooking.
6. After 3-4 minutes, carefully shake the basket or flip the shrimp using tongs to ensure even cooking.
7. Continue cooking for another 3-4 minutes or until the shrimp are pink and opaque.
8. Once cooked, remove the shrimp from the air fryer and transfer them to a serving plate.
9. Serve the **Garlic Parmesan Shrimp** immediately with lemon wedges on the side for squeezing over the shrimp and garnish with chopped parsley if desired.

## Lemon Pepper Shrimp

🕐 **Cooking Time: 8 Min**  🍴 **Servings: 2-3**

- 300g large shrimp, peeled and deveined
- 2 tbsp olive oil
- 2 cloves garlic, minced
- Zest of 1 lemon
- 1/2 tsp black pepper
- Salt to taste
- Lemon wedges for serving (optional)
- Chopped parsley for garnish (optional)

## Teriyaki Chicken

🕐 **Cooking Time: 20 Min**  🍴 **Servings: 4**

- 500g boneless, skinless chicken thighs, cut into bite-sized pieces
- 4 tbsp soy sauce
- 2 tbsp mirin
- 2 tbsp sake (or dry sherry)
- 2 tbsp brown sugar
- 1 tbsp honey
- 2 cloves garlic, minced
- 1 tsp grated ginger
- 1 tbsp cornstarch
- 1 tbsp water
- Sesame seeds and chopped spring onions for garnish (optional)

---

## INSTRUCTION

---

1. In a bowl, combine the olive oil, minced garlic, lemon zest, black pepper, and salt.
2. Add the peeled and deveined shrimp to the bowl and toss until the shrimp are evenly coated with the mixture.
3. Lightly grease Zone 1 of the air fryer basket with cooking oil spray. Place the coated shrimp in Zone 1, ensuring they are in a single layer and not too crowded.
4. Select Zone 1, choose the AIR FRY program, and set the temperature to 200°C. Set the time to 6-8 minutes.
5. Press the START/STOP button to begin cooking.
6. After 3-4 minutes, carefully shake the basket or flip the shrimp using tongs to ensure even cooking.
7. Continue cooking for another 3-4 minutes or until the shrimp are pink and opaque.
8. Once cooked, remove the shrimp from the air fryer and transfer them to a serving plate.
9. Serve the **Lemon Pepper Shrimp** immediately with lemon wedges on the side for squeezing over the shrimp and garnish with chopped parsley if desired.

1. In a bowl, mix together the soy sauce, mirin, sake, brown sugar, honey, minced garlic, and grated ginger.
2. Add the chicken pieces to the bowl and marinate for about 15-20 minutes.
3. In a small bowl, mix the cornstarch with water to make a slurry.
4. Lightly grease Zone 1 of the air fryer basket with cooking oil spray. Place the marinated chicken pieces in Zone 1, ensuring they are in a single layer and not too crowded.
5. Select Zone 1, choose the AIR FRY program, and set the temperature to 180°C. Set the time to 15-18 minutes.
6. Press the START/STOP button to begin cooking.
7. After 8-10 minutes, carefully flip the chicken pieces using tongs to ensure even cooking.
8. Continue cooking for another 7-8 minutes or until the chicken is cooked through and the sauce has thickened.
9. Once cooked, remove the **chicken** from the air fryer and transfer it to a serving plate.
10. Garnish with sesame seeds and chopped spring onions if desired.

# BBQ Chicken

🕐 **Cooking Time: 20 Min**  🍴 **Servings: 4**

- 4 boneless, skinless chicken breasts
- 200ml BBQ sauce
- 1 tbsp olive oil
- 1 tsp smoked paprika
- 1/2 tsp garlic powder
- Salt and pepper to taste
- Chopped parsley for garnish (optional)

# Cheese-Walnut Stuffed Mushrooms

🕐 **Cooking Time: 15 Min**  🍴 **Servings: 4**

- 8 large button mushrooms
- 50g grated cheddar cheese
- 25g breadcrumbs
- 25g chopped walnuts
- 1 tablespoon chopped fresh parsley
- 1 clove garlic, minced
- 1 tablespoon olive oil
- Salt and pepper to taste.

## INSTRUCTION

1. In a bowl, mix together the BBQ sauce, olive oil, smoked paprika, garlic powder, salt, and pepper.
2. Add the chicken breasts to the bowl and toss until they are evenly coated with the BBQ sauce mixture.
3. Lightly grease Zone 1 of the air fryer basket with cooking oil spray. Place the coated chicken breasts in Zone 1, ensuring they are in a single layer and not too crowded.
4. Select Zone 1, choose the AIR FRY program, and set the temperature to 180°C. Set the time to 18-20 minutes.
5. Press the START/STOP button to begin cooking.
6. After 10-12 minutes, carefully flip the chicken breasts using tongs to ensure even cooking.
7. Continue cooking for another 8-10 minutes or until the chicken is cooked through and the sauce is caramelized.
8. Once cooked, remove the **chicken** from the air fryer and transfer it to a serving plate.
9. Garnish with chopped parsley if desired.

1. Remove the stems from the mushrooms and set them aside.
2. In a mixing bowl, combine the grated cheddar cheese, breadcrumbs, chopped walnuts, chopped parsley, minced garlic, olive oil, salt, and pepper. Mix well to form a stuffing mixture.
3. Fill each mushroom cap with a generous amount of the cheese-walnut stuffing mixture, pressing it gently to ensure it stays in place.
4. Finely chop the reserved mushroom stems and distribute them evenly over the stuffed mushrooms.
5. Place the stuffed mushrooms in Zone 1 of the Ninja Dual Zone air fryer. Make sure they are arranged in a single layer.
6. Select Zone 1, choose the AIR FRY function, set the temperature to 180°C. Time to 12 minutes, until the mushrooms are tender and the cheese is melted and lightly golden.
7. Once cooked, carefully remove the stuffed mushrooms from the air fryer and let them cool for a few minutes before serving.
8. Serve the **Cheese-Walnut Stuffed Mushrooms** as a delicious appetizer or side dish.

# Potato with Creamy Cheese

⏱ **Cooking Time:** 30 Min  🍴 **Servings:** 2

- 2 large potatoes, washed and thinly sliced
- 100g grated cheddar cheese
- 60ml sour cream
- 30g butter, melted
- 2 tablespoons chopped fresh chives
- Salt and pepper to taste.

# Traditional Queso Fundido

⏱ **Cooking Time:** 15 Min  🍴 **Servings:** 4

- 200g grated Cheddar cheese
- 200g grated Monterey Jack cheese
- 1 tablespoon olive oil
- 1 small onion, finely chopped
- 2 cloves garlic, minced
- 1 jalapeno pepper, seeded and finely chopped
- 1/2 teaspoon ground cumin
- 1/2 teaspoon paprika
- Salt and pepper, to taste
- Tortilla chips, for serving

## INSTRUCTION

1. In a bowl, combine the grated cheddar cheese, sour cream, melted butter, chopped fresh chives, salt, and pepper. Mix well to create a creamy cheese mixture.
2. Place the thinly sliced potatoes in a separate bowl and season them with salt and pepper.
3. Take one potato slice and spread a layer of the creamy cheese mixture on top. Place another potato slice on top and repeat the process until you have a stack of potato slices with the cheese mixture in between.
4. Repeat the process for the remaining potato slices and cheese mixture, creating multiple potato stacks.
5. Lightly grease the air fryer basket in Zone 1 of Air Fryer.
6. Place the potato stacks in a single layer in the greased air fryer basket.
7. Select Zone 1, choose the AIR FRY function, and set the temperature to 180°C, cooking time to 30 minutes. Press the START/STOP.
8. After the cooking time is complete, carefully remove the Potato with Creamy Cheese stacks from the air fryer using tongs or a spatula.
9. Serve the **Potato with Creamy Cheese** as a delightful side dish or as a main course. The potatoes will be crispy on the outside and tender on the inside, complemented by the creamy and cheesy filling.

1. In a skillet, heat the vegetable oil over medium heat. Add the diced onion and jalapeño pepper (if using) and sauté until softened, about 3-4 minutes. Add the minced garlic to the skillet and sauté for an additional minute.
2. Add the diced tomatoes to the skillet and cook for 2-3 minutes, stirring occasionally, until the tomatoes are heated through.
3. In Zone 1, place the grated Cheddar cheese and Monterey Jack cheese in an even layer.
4. Insert the air fryer basket into Air Fryer. Select Zone 1, choosing AIR FRY and setting the temperature to 180°C in 5 minutes. This will melt the cheese and create a gooey base.
5. After 5 minutes, carefully remove the air fryer basket and top the melted cheese with the sautéed onion, jalapeño, garlic, and diced tomatoes.
6. Return the air fryer basket to Zone 1 of the air fryer and continue cooking for an additional 5 minutes or until the cheese is fully melted and bubbling.
7. Once done, remove the air fryer basket from the Ninja Dual Zone Air Fryer and sprinkle the chopped fresh cilantro over the melted cheese.
8. Season with salt and pepper to taste.
9. Serve the **Traditional Queso Fundido** immediately with tortilla chips for dipping.

# Garlic Parmesan Chicken

🕐 **Cooking Time:** 20 Min  🍴 **Servings:** 4

- 4 boneless, skinless chicken breasts (about 150g each)
- 30g grated Parmesan cheese
- 30g breadcrumbs
- 1 teaspoon dried oregano
- 1/2 teaspoon salt
- 1/2 teaspoon black pepper
- 1 tablespoon olive oil
- 2 cloves garlic, minced
- Cooking spray or oil for greasing

# Lemon Pepper Chicken Breasts

🕐 **Cooking Time:** 20 Min  🍴 **Servings:** 4

- 4 boneless, skinless chicken breasts (about 150g each)
- 2 tablespoons olive oil
- Zest of 1 lemon
- 1 tablespoon lemon juice
- 1 teaspoon ground black pepper
- 1 teaspoon garlic powder
- 1/2 teaspoon salt
- Cooking spray or oil for greasing

## INSTRUCTION

1. In a small bowl, mix together the Parmesan cheese, breadcrumbs, dried oregano, salt, and black pepper.
2. In another bowl, mix the olive oil and minced garlic.
3. Dip each chicken breast into the garlic oil mixture, ensuring it's coated evenly.
4. Coat the chicken breasts with the breadcrumb mixture, pressing gently to adhere the mixture to the chicken.
5. Lightly spray or brush the Zone 1 with cooking spray or oil to prevent sticking.
6. Place the coated chicken breasts in Zone 1 of the Ninja Dual Zone Air Fryer, ensuring they are arranged in a single layer.
7. Select Zone 1, choose the AIR FRY program, and set the temperature to 180°C. Set the time to 20 minutes.
8. Press the START/STOP button to begin cooking.
9. Check the chicken after 15 minutes to see if it's golden brown and crispy. If not, continue cooking for the remaining time.
10. Once done, carefully remove the chicken from the air fryer and let it rest for a few minutes before serving.
11. Serve the **Garlic Parmesan Chicken** hot with your favorite sides or salad.

1. In a small bowl, mix together the olive oil, lemon zest, lemon juice, ground black pepper, garlic powder, and salt.
2. Place the chicken breasts in a shallow dish and pour the lemon pepper marinade over them, ensuring they are evenly coated. Let them marinate for 10-15 minutes.
3. Lightly spray or brush the Zone 1 with cooking spray or oil to prevent sticking.
4. Place the marinated chicken breasts in Zone 1 of the Ninja Dual Zone Air Fryer, ensuring they are arranged in a single layer.
5. Select Zone 1, choose the AIR FRY program, and set the temperature to 180°C. Set the time to 20 minutes.
6. Press the START/STOP button to begin cooking.
7. Check the chicken after 15 minutes to see if it's cooked through and the skin is crispy. If not, continue cooking for the remaining time.
8. Once done, carefully remove the chicken from the air fryer and let it rest for a few minutes before serving.
9. Serve the **Lemon Pepper Chicken Breasts** hot with your favorite sides or salad.

# Teriyaki Chicken Skewers

🕐 **Cooking Time: 20 Min**  🍴 **Servings: 4**

- 4 boneless, skinless chicken breasts (about 150g each), cut into cubes
- 120ml teriyaki sauce
- 2 tablespoons honey
- 1 tablespoon soy sauce
- 1 tablespoon rice vinegar
- 1 teaspoon minced garlic
- 1 teaspoon minced ginger
- 1/2 teaspoon sesame oil
- Sesame seeds and chopped spring onions for garnish (optional)
- Wooden skewers, soaked in water for 30 minutes

# Southern Fried Chicken

🕐 **Cooking Time: 25 Min**  🍴 **Servings: 4**

- 8 pieces of chicken (a mix of thighs and drumsticks)
- 120g all-purpose flour
- 1 teaspoon salt
- 1 teaspoon paprika
- 1/2 teaspoon garlic powder
- 1/2 teaspoon onion powder
- 1/2 teaspoon black pepper
- 1/2 teaspoon dried thyme
- 1/2 teaspoon dried oregano
- 2 eggs
- 2 tablespoons milk
- Cooking spray or oil for greasing

## INSTRUCTION

1. In a bowl, mix together the teriyaki sauce, honey, soy sauce, rice vinegar, minced garlic, minced ginger, and sesame oil to make the marinade.
2. Thread the chicken pieces onto the soaked wooden skewers.
3. Place the chicken skewers in Zone 1 of the Ninja Dual Zone Air Fryer, ensuring they are arranged in a single layer.
4. Select Zone 1, choose the AIR FRY program, and set the temperature to 180°C. Set the time to 10 minutes.
5. Press the START/STOP button to begin cooking.
6. After 10 minutes, carefully turn the skewers over and brush them with some of the remaining marinade.
7. Continue cooking for another 10 minutes or until the chicken is cooked through and caramelized, basting with the marinade occasionally.
8. Once done, carefully remove the chicken skewers from the air fryer and let them rest for a few minutes.
9. Garnish with sesame seeds and chopped spring onions if desired.
10. Serve the **Teriyaki Chicken Skewers** hot with steamed rice and vegetables.

1. In a shallow dish, mix together the flour, salt, paprika, garlic powder, onion powder, black pepper, thyme, and oregano.
2. In another dish, whisk together the eggs and milk to create an egg wash.
3. Dip each piece of chicken into the egg wash, then dredge it in the seasoned flour mixture, ensuring it's evenly coated.
4. Lightly spray or brush both air fryer basket with cooking spray or oil to prevent sticking.
5. Evenly dividing coated chicken pieces between the two zone, ensuring they are arranged in a single layer.
6. Select Zone 1, choose the AIR FRY program, and set the temperature to 180°C. Set the time to 25 minutes. Select MATCH to duplicate settings across both zones. Press the START/STOP.
7. After 15 minutes, flip the chicken pieces over to ensure even cooking. Continue cooking for the remaining time or until the chicken is golden brown and crispy.
8. Once done, carefully remove the chicken from the air fryer and let it rest for a few minutes.
9. Serve the **Southern Fried Chicken** hot with your favorite sides like mashed potatoes, coleslaw, or cornbread.

## Buffalo Chicken Tenders

🕐 **Cooking Time: 20 Min**   🍴 **Servings: 4**

- 500g chicken breast tenders
- 60g all-purpose flour
- 1/2 teaspoon salt
- 1/2 teaspoon garlic powder
- 1/2 teaspoon paprika
- 1/4 teaspoon black pepper
- 2 eggs
- 60ml hot sauce (such as Frank's RedHot)
- 60g breadcrumbs
- Cooking spray or oil for greasing

## Herb-Crusted Turkey Wings

🕐 **Cooking Time: 30 Min**   🍴 **Servings: 4**

- 4 turkey wings
- 30g breadcrumbs
- 20g grated Parmesan cheese
- 1 teaspoon dried thyme
- 1 teaspoon dried rosemary
- 1 teaspoon dried sage
- 1/2 teaspoon garlic powder
- 1/2 teaspoon onion powder
- 1/2 teaspoon salt
- 1/2 teaspoon black pepper
- 2 tablespoons olive oil
- Cooking spray or oil for greasing

## INSTRUCTION

1. In a shallow dish, mix together the all-purpose flour, salt, garlic powder, paprika, and black pepper.
2. In another dish, beat the eggs and mix in the hot sauce to create a spicy egg wash.
3. Place the breadcrumbs in a third dish.
4. Dredge each chicken tender in the seasoned flour mixture, then dip it into the spicy egg wash, and finally coat it with breadcrumbs, pressing gently to adhere.
5. Lightly spray or brush the Zone 1 with cooking spray or oil to prevent sticking.
6. Place the coated chicken tenders in Zone 1 of the Ninja Dual Zone Air Fryer, ensuring they are arranged in a single layer.
7. Select Zone 1, choose the AIR FRY program, and set the temperature to 180°C. Set the time to 10 minutes.
8. Press the START/STOP button to begin cooking.
9. After 10 minutes, carefully turn the chicken tenders over and continue cooking for another 8-10 minutes or until they are golden brown and crispy.
10. Once done, carefully remove the chicken tenders from the air fryer and let them rest for a few minutes.
11. Serve the **Buffalo Chicken Tenders** hot with celery sticks and ranch or blue cheese dressing for dipping.

1. In a bowl, combine the breadcrumbs, grated Parmesan cheese, dried thyme, dried rosemary, dried sage, garlic powder, onion powder, salt, and black pepper.
2. Rub the turkey wings with olive oil.
3. Coat each turkey wing with the herb and breadcrumb mixture, pressing gently to adhere the mixture to the wings.
4. Lightly spray or brush the Zone 1 with cooking spray or oil to prevent sticking.
5. Place the coated turkey wings in Zone 1 of the Ninja Dual Zone Air Fryer, ensuring they are arranged in a single layer.
6. Select Zone 1, choose the AIR FRY program, and set the temperature to 180°C. Set the time to 30 minutes.
7. Press the START/STOP button to begin cooking.
8. After 15 minutes, flip the turkey wings over for even cooking.
9. Continue cooking for the remaining time or until the turkey wings are golden brown and crispy.
10. Once done, carefully remove the turkey wings from the air fryer and let them rest for a few minutes. Serve the **Herb-Crusted Turkey Wings** hot with your favorite sides

## Soy Ginger Duck Breast

⏱ **Cooking Time:** 15 Min  🍽 **Servings:** 2

- 2 duck breasts (about 250g each)
- 60ml soy sauce
- 2 tablespoons honey
- 1 tablespoon rice vinegar
- 1 tablespoon grated fresh ginger
- 1 clove garlic, minced
- 1/2 teaspoon sesame oil
- 1/4 teaspoon black pepper
- Cooking spray or oil for greasing

## Crispy Quail

⏱ **Cooking Time:** 20 Min  🍽 **Servings:** 2

- 4 whole quails
- 60g all-purpose flour
- 1 teaspoon garlic powder
- 1 teaspoon onion powder
- 1 teaspoon paprika
- 1/2 teaspoon salt
- 1/2 teaspoon black pepper
- 2 eggs
- 60ml milk
- Cooking spray or oil for greasing

---

## INSTRUCTION

---

1. In a bowl, whisk together the soy sauce, honey, rice vinegar, grated ginger, minced garlic, sesame oil, and black pepper to make the marinade.
2. Score the skin of the duck breasts with a sharp knife in a criss-cross pattern, being careful not to cut into the meat.
3. Place the duck breasts in a shallow dish and pour the marinade over them, ensuring they are evenly coated. Let them marinate for 10-15 minutes.
4. Lightly spray or brush the air fryer basket with cooking spray or oil to prevent sticking.
5. Place the duck breasts in Zone 1 of the Ninja Dual Zone Air Fryer, ensuring they are arranged in a single layer.
6. Select Zone 1, choose the AIR FRY program, and set the temperature to 180°C. Set the time to 15 minutes.
7. Press the START/STOP button to begin cooking.
8. After 8 minutes, carefully turn the duck breasts over for even cooking.
9. Continue cooking for the remaining time or until the duck breasts are cooked to your desired level of doneness and the skin is crispy.
10. Once done, carefully remove the duck breasts from the air fryer and let them rest for a few minutes.
11. Slice the **duck breasts** and serve them hot with your favorite side dishes.

---

1. In a shallow dish, mix together the all-purpose flour, garlic powder, onion powder, paprika, salt, and black pepper.
2. In another dish, whisk together the eggs and milk to create an egg wash.
3. Pat the quails dry with paper towels.
4. Dredge each quail in the seasoned flour mixture, then dip it into the egg wash, and finally coat it with another layer of seasoned flour mixture, pressing gently to adhere.
5. Lightly spray or brush the Zone 1 with cooking spray or oil to prevent sticking.
6. Place the coated quails in Zone 1 of the Ninja Dual Zone Air Fryer, ensuring they are arranged in a single layer.
7. Select Zone 1, choose the AIR FRY program, and set the temperature to 180°C. Set the time to 20 minutes.
8. Press the START/STOP button to begin cooking.
9. After 10 minutes, carefully turn the quails over for even cooking.
10. Continue cooking for the remaining time or until the quails are golden brown and crispy.
11. Once done, carefully remove the quails from the air fryer and let them rest for a few minutes.
12. Serve the **Crispy Quail** hot with your favorite sides or dipping sauce.

## Orange Glazed Chicken

🕐 **Cooking Time: 25 Min**  🍴 **Servings: 4**

- 4 boneless, skinless chicken breasts (about 150g each)
- 120ml orange juice
- Zest of 1 orange
- 2 tablespoons soy sauce
- 2 tablespoons honey
- 1 tablespoon rice vinegar
- 1 teaspoon grated fresh ginger
- 1 clove garlic, minced
- 1/2 teaspoon sesame oil
- 1/4 teaspoon black pepper
- Cooking spray or oil for greasing

## Maple Dijon Chicken Thighs

🕐 **Cooking Time: 25 Min**  🍴 **Servings: 4**

- 8 bone-in, skin-on chicken thighs
- 60ml maple syrup
- 2 tablespoons Dijon mustard
- 1 tablespoon soy sauce
- 1 tablespoon olive oil
- 1 teaspoon minced garlic
- 1/2 teaspoon dried thyme
- 1/2 teaspoon salt
- 1/4 teaspoon black pepper
- Cooking spray or oil for greasing

## INSTRUCTION

1. In a bowl, whisk together the orange juice, orange zest, soy sauce, honey, rice vinegar, grated ginger, minced garlic, sesame oil, and black pepper to make the glaze.
2. Pat the chicken breasts dry with paper towels.
3. Lightly spray or brush the Zone 1 with cooking spray or oil to prevent sticking.
4. Place the chicken breasts in Zone 1 of the Ninja Dual Zone Air Fryer, ensuring they are arranged in a single layer.
5. Select Zone 1, choose the AIR FRY program, and set the temperature to 180°C. Set the time to 20 minutes.
6. Press the START/STOP button to begin cooking.
7. After 15 minutes, carefully brush the chicken breasts with the prepared orange glaze.
8. Continue cooking for the remaining time or until the chicken is cooked through and the glaze is sticky and caramelized.
9. Once done, carefully remove the chicken breasts from the air fryer and let them rest for a few minutes.
10. Serve the **Orange Glazed Chicken** hot with steamed rice and vegetables.

1. In a bowl, whisk together the maple syrup, Dijon mustard, soy sauce, olive oil, minced garlic, dried thyme, salt, and black pepper to make the marinade.
2. Pat the chicken thighs dry with paper towels.
3. Place the chicken thighs in a shallow dish and pour the marinade over them, ensuring they are evenly coated. Let them marinate for 10-15 minutes.
4. Lightly spray or brush the both basket with cooking spray or oil to prevent sticking.
5. Place the marinated chicken thighs in two Zone of the Ninja Dual Zone Air Fryer, ensuring they are arranged in a single layer.
6. Select Zone 1, choose the AIR FRY program, and set the temperature to 180°C. Set the time to 25 minutes. Select MATCH to duplicate settings across both zones. Press the START/STOP.
7. After 15 minutes, carefully turn the chicken thighs over for even cooking.
8. Continue cooking for the remaining time or until the chicken thighs are cooked through and the skin is crispy and caramelized.
9. Once done, carefully remove the chicken thighs from the air fryer and let them rest for a few minutes.
10. Serve the **Maple Dijon Chicken Thighs** hot with your favorite sides.

# Peri-Peri Chicken

🕐 Cooking Time: 20 Min  🍴 Servings: 4

- 8 bone-in, skin-on chicken thighs
- 60ml olive oil
- 2 tablespoons lemon juice
- 2 tablespoons red wine vinegar
- 2 cloves garlic, minced
- 1 teaspoon smoked paprika
- 1 teaspoon dried oregano
- 1 teaspoon ground cumin
- 1/2 teaspoon cayenne pepper (adjust to taste)
- 1/2 teaspoon salt
- 1/4 teaspoon black pepper
- Cooking spray or oil for greasing

# Sesame Ginger Chicken Wings

🕐 Cooking Time: 20 Min  🍴 Servings: 4

- 1 kg chicken wings, separated into wingettes and drumettes
- 2 tablespoons soy sauce
- 2 tablespoons hoisin sauce
- 1 tablespoon honey
- 1 tablespoon sesame oil
- 1 tablespoon grated fresh ginger
- 2 cloves garlic, minced
- 1 teaspoon rice vinegar
- 1/2 teaspoon red pepper flakes (optional)
- 1 tablespoon sesame seeds
- Chopped spring onions for garnish (optional)
- Cooking spray or oil for greasing

## INSTRUCTION

1. In a bowl, whisk together the olive oil, lemon juice, red wine vinegar, minced garlic, smoked paprika, dried oregano, ground cumin, cayenne pepper, salt, and black pepper to make the peri-peri marinade.
2. Pat the chicken thighs dry with paper towels.
3. Place the chicken thighs in a shallow dish and pour the peri-peri marinade over them, ensuring they are evenly coated. Let them marinate for 10-15 minutes.
4. Lightly spray or brush both basket with cooking spray or oil to prevent sticking.
5. Place the marinated chicken thighs in two Zone of the Ninja Dual Zone Air Fryer, ensuring they are arranged in a single layer.
6. Select Zone 1, choose the AIR FRY program, and set the temperature to 180°C. Set the time to 20 minutes. Select MATCH. Press the START/STOP.
7. After 10 minutes, carefully turn the chicken thighs over for even cooking.
8. Continue cooking for the remaining time or until the chicken thighs are cooked through and the skin is crispy and charred in places.
9. Once done, carefully remove the chicken thighs from the air fryer and let them rest for a few minutes. Serve the **Peri-Peri Chicken** hot with your favorite sides.

1. In a bowl, whisk together the soy sauce, hoisin sauce, honey, sesame oil, grated ginger, minced garlic, rice vinegar, and red pepper flakes (if using) to make the marinade.
2. Place the chicken wings in a large resealable plastic bag or a bowl. Pour the marinade over the chicken wings, ensuring they are evenly coated. Marinate for at least 30 minutes in the refrigerator.
3. Lightly spray or brush the both basket with cooking spray or oil to prevent sticking.
4. Place the marinated chicken wings in two Zone of the Ninja Dual Zone Air Fryer, ensuring they are arranged in a single layer.
5. Select Zone 1, choose the AIR FRY program, and set the temperature to 180°C. Set the time to 20 minutes. Select MATCH. Press the START/STOP.
6. After 10 minutes, carefully turn the chicken wings over for even cooking.
7. Continue cooking for the remaining time or until the chicken wings are cooked through and crispy.
8. Once done, carefully remove the chicken wings from the air fryer and place them on a serving platter.
9. Sprinkle the **sesame seeds** and chopped spring onions (if using) over the **chicken wings**.

## Pesto Parmesan Chicken

⏱ **Cooking Time:** 20 Min  🍽 **Servings:** 4

- 4 boneless, skinless chicken breasts (about 150g each)
- 60g store-bought or homemade pesto sauce
- 40g grated Parmesan cheese
- 40g breadcrumbs
- 1/2 teaspoon garlic powder
- 1/2 teaspoon onion powder
- 1/2 teaspoon salt
- 1/4 teaspoon black pepper
- Cooking spray or oil for greasing

## Spicy Sriracha Chicken

⏱ **Cooking Time:** 20 Min  🍽 **Servings:** 4

- 4 boneless, skinless chicken breasts (about 150g each)
- 60ml sriracha sauce
- 2 tablespoons honey
- 2 tablespoons soy sauce
- 1 tablespoon rice vinegar
- 1 teaspoon sesame oil
- 1 teaspoon grated fresh ginger
- 1 clove garlic, minced
- 1/2 teaspoon red pepper flakes (adjust to taste)
- Cooking spray or oil for greasing

## INSTRUCTION

1. In a shallow dish, mix together the grated Parmesan cheese, breadcrumbs, garlic powder, onion powder, salt, and black pepper.
2. Spread a thin layer of pesto sauce on each chicken breast.
3. Dredge each pesto-coated chicken breast in the breadcrumb mixture, pressing gently to adhere the mixture to the chicken.
4. Lightly spray or brush the Zone 1 air fryer basket with cooking spray to prevent sticking.
5. Place the coated chicken breasts in Zone 1 of the Ninja Dual Zone Air Fryer, ensuring they are arranged in a single layer.
6. Select Zone 1, choose the AIR FRY program, and set the temperature to 180°C. Set the time to 20 minutes.
7. Press the START/STOP button to begin cooking.
8. After 10 minutes, carefully turn the chicken breasts over for even cooking.
9. Continue cooking for the remaining time or until the chicken breasts are cooked through and the coating is golden and crispy.
10. Once done, carefully remove the chicken breasts from the air fryer and let them rest for a few minutes.
11. Serve the **Pesto Parmesan Chicken** hot with a side salad or your favorite vegetables.

1. In a bowl, whisk together the sriracha sauce, honey, soy sauce, rice vinegar, sesame oil, grated ginger, minced garlic, and red pepper flakes to make the spicy marinade.
2. Pat the chicken breasts dry with paper towels.
3. Place the chicken breasts in a shallow dish and pour the spicy marinade over them, ensuring they are evenly coated. Let them marinate for 10-15 minutes.
4. Lightly spray or brush the Zone 1 air fryer basket with cooking spray to prevent sticking.
5. Place the marinated chicken breasts in Zone 1 of the Ninja Dual Zone Air Fryer, ensuring they are arranged in a single layer.
6. Select Zone 1, choose the AIR FRY program, and set the temperature to 180°C. Set the time to 20 minutes.
7. Press the START/STOP button to begin cooking.
8. After 10 minutes, carefully turn the chicken breasts over for even cooking.
9. Continue cooking for the remaining time or until the chicken breasts are cooked through and the exterior is caramelized.
10. Once done, carefully remove the chicken breasts from the air fryer and let them rest for a few minutes.
11. Serve the **Spicy Sriracha Chicken** hot with steamed rice and vegetables.

# Lime & Cilantro Chicken

**Cooking Time:** 20 Min  **Servings:** 4

- 4 boneless, skinless chicken breasts (about 150g each)
- Zest and juice of 2 limes
- 2 tablespoons chopped fresh cilantro (coriander)
- 2 tablespoons olive oil
- 2 cloves garlic, minced
- 1/2 teaspoon ground cumin
- 1/2 teaspoon salt
- 1/4 teaspoon black pepper
- Cooking spray or oil for greasing

# Garlic Butter Chicken Breast

**Cooking Time:** 20 Min  **Servings:** 4

- 4 boneless, skinless chicken breasts (about 150g each)
- 60g unsalted butter, melted
- 4 cloves garlic, minced
- 1 tablespoon chopped fresh parsley
- 1/2 teaspoon salt
- 1/4 teaspoon black pepper
- Cooking spray or oil for greasing

## INSTRUCTION

1. In a bowl, whisk together the lime zest, lime juice, chopped cilantro, olive oil, minced garlic, ground cumin, salt, and black pepper to make the marinade.
2. Pat the chicken breasts dry with paper towels.
3. Place the chicken breasts in a shallow dish and pour the marinade over them, ensuring they are evenly coated. Let them marinate for 10-15 minutes.
4. Lightly spray or brush the Zone 1 basket with cooking spray or oil to prevent sticking.
5. Place the marinated chicken breasts in Zone 1 of the Ninja Dual Zone Air Fryer, ensuring they are arranged in a single layer.
6. Select Zone 1, choose the AIR FRY program, and set the temperature to 180°C. Set the time to 20 minutes.
7. Press the START/STOP button to begin cooking.
8. After 10 minutes, carefully turn the chicken breasts over for even cooking.
9. Continue cooking for the remaining time or until the chicken breasts are cooked through and the exterior is golden and slightly crispy.
10. Once done, carefully remove the chicken breasts from the air fryer and let them rest for a few minutes.
11. Serve the **Lime and Cilantro Chicken** hot with a fresh salad or your favorite side dishes.

1. In a bowl, mix together the melted butter, minced garlic, chopped parsley, salt, and black pepper to make the garlic butter mixture.
2. Pat the chicken breasts dry with paper towels.
3. Place the chicken breasts in a shallow dish and pour the garlic butter mixture over them, ensuring they are evenly coated. Let them marinate for 10 minutes.
4. Lightly spray or brush the Zone 1 basket with cooking spray or oil to prevent sticking.
5. Place the marinated chicken breasts in Zone 1 of the Ninja Dual Zone Air Fryer, ensuring they are arranged in a single layer.
6. Select Zone 1, choose the AIR FRY program, and set the temperature to 180°C. Set the time to 20 minutes.
7. Press the START/STOP button to begin cooking.
8. After 10 minutes, carefully turn the chicken breasts over for even cooking.
9. Continue cooking for the remaining time or until the chicken breasts are cooked through and the exterior is golden and slightly crispy.
10. Once done, carefully remove the chicken breasts from the air fryer and let them rest for a few minutes.
11. Serve the **Garlic Butter Chicken Breast** hot with your favorite sides.

# Crispy Coconut Chicken Strips

🕐 **Cooking Time: 15 Min**   🍴 **Servings: 4**

- 500g boneless, skinless chicken breasts, cut into strips
- 2 eggs
- 60g all-purpose flour
- 100g shredded coconut
- 50g panko breadcrumbs
- 1/2 teaspoon salt
- 1/4 teaspoon black pepper
- Cooking spray or oil for greasing

# Mango Chili Turkey Breast

🕐 **Cooking Time: 25 Min**   🍴 **Servings: 4**

- 4 turkey breast fillets (about 150g each)
- 1 ripe mango, peeled and diced
- 2 tablespoons honey
- 1 tablespoon soy sauce
- 1 tablespoon lime juice
- 1 teaspoon chili flakes (adjust to taste)
- 1/2 teaspoon ground cumin
- 1/2 teaspoon ground coriander
- 1/2 teaspoon salt
- Cooking spray or oil for greasing

## INSTRUCTION

1. In a shallow dish, whisk the eggs.
2. In another shallow dish, mix together the all-purpose flour, shredded coconut, panko breadcrumbs, salt, and black pepper.
3. Dip each chicken strip into the beaten eggs, then dredge it in the coconut mixture, pressing gently to coat evenly.
4. Lightly spray or brush the Zone 1 air fryer basket with cooking spray or oil to prevent sticking.
5. Place the coated chicken strips in Zone 1 of the Ninja Dual Zone Air Fryer, ensuring they are arranged in a single layer.
6. Select Zone 1, choose the AIR FRY program, and set the temperature to 200°C. Set the time to 15 minutes.
7. Press the START/STOP button to begin cooking.
8. After 8 minutes, carefully turn the chicken strips over for even cooking.
9. Continue cooking for the remaining time or until the chicken strips are golden brown and crispy.
10. Once done, carefully remove the chicken strips from the air fryer and let them cool for a few minutes.
11. Serve the **Crispy Coconut Chicken Strips** hot with your favorite dipping sauce.

---

1. In a blender or food processor, blend the diced mango, honey, soy sauce, lime juice, chili flakes, ground cumin, ground coriander, and salt until smooth to make the mango chili marinade.
2. Place the turkey breast fillets in a shallow dish and pour the mango chili marinade over them, ensuring they are evenly coated. Let them marinate for 15-20 minutes.
3. Lightly spray or brush the Zone 1 air fryer basket with cooking spray or oil to prevent sticking.
4. Place the marinated turkey breast fillets in Zone 1 of the Ninja Dual Zone Air Fryer, ensuring they are arranged in a single layer.
5. Select Zone 1, choose the AIR FRY program, and set the temperature to 180°C. Set the time to 25 minutes.
6. Press the START/STOP button to begin cooking.
7. After 15 minutes, carefully turn the turkey breast fillets over for even cooking.
8. Continue cooking for the remaining time or until the turkey breast fillets are cooked through and the exterior is caramelized.
9. Once done, carefully remove the turkey breast fillets from the air fryer and let them rest for a few minutes.
10. Serve the **Mango Chili Turkey Breast** hot with a side salad or your favorite sides.

# Pesto Crusted Chicken

⏱ **Cooking Time:** 20 Min   🍴 **Servings:** 4

- 4 boneless, skinless chicken breasts (about 150g each)
- 120g pesto sauce (store-bought or homemade)
- 60g breadcrumbs
- 30g grated Parmesan cheese
- 1/2 teaspoon garlic powder
- 1/2 teaspoon onion powder
- 1/2 teaspoon salt
- 1/4 teaspoon black pepper
- Cooking spray or oil for greasing

# Thyme & Garlic Chicken

⏱ **Cooking Time:** 20 Min   🍴 **Servings:** 4

- 4 boneless, skinless chicken breasts (about 150g each)
- 4 cloves garlic, minced
- 2 tablespoons olive oil
- 2 tablespoons fresh thyme leaves
- 1/2 teaspoon salt
- 1/4 teaspoon black pepper
- Cooking spray or oil for greasing

## INSTRUCTION

1. In a bowl, mix together the breadcrumbs, grated Parmesan cheese, garlic powder, onion powder, salt, and black pepper to make the crust mixture.
2. Pat the chicken breasts dry with paper towels.
3. Spread a layer of pesto sauce over each chicken breast.
4. Press the pesto-coated side of each chicken breast into the crust mixture, ensuring the chicken is evenly coated.
5. Lightly spray or brush the Zone 1 air fryer basket with cooking spray or oil to prevent sticking.
6. Place the coated chicken breasts in Zone 1 of the Ninja Dual Zone Air Fryer, ensuring they are arranged in a single layer.
7. Select Zone 1, choose the AIR FRY program, and set the temperature to 180°C. Set the time to 20 minutes.
8. Press the START/STOP button to begin cooking.
9. After 10 minutes, carefully turn the chicken breasts over for even cooking.
10. Continue cooking for the remaining time or until the chicken breasts are cooked through and the crust is golden and crispy.
11. Once done, carefully remove the chicken breasts from the air fryer and let them rest for a few minutes.
12. Serve the **Pesto Crusted Chicken** hot with your favorite sides.

1. In a small bowl, mix together the minced garlic, olive oil, fresh thyme leaves, salt, and black pepper to make the marinade.
2. Pat the chicken breasts dry with paper towels.
3. Rub the garlic and thyme marinade over both sides of each chicken breast, ensuring they are evenly coated.
4. Lightly spray or brush the air fryer basket with cooking spray or oil to prevent sticking.
5. Place the marinated chicken breasts in Zone 1 of the Ninja Dual Zone Air Fryer, ensuring they are arranged in a single layer.
6. Select Zone 1, choose the AIR FRY program, and set the temperature to 180°C. Set the time to 20 minutes.
7. Press the START/STOP button to begin cooking.
8. After 10 minutes, carefully turn the chicken breasts over for even cooking.
9. Continue cooking for the remaining time or until the chicken breasts are cooked through and the exterior is golden and slightly crispy.
10. Once done, carefully remove the chicken breasts from the air fryer and let them rest for a few minutes.
11. Serve the **Thyme and Garlic Chicken** hot with your favorite sides.

# Tandoori Spiced Chicken

🕐 **Cooking Time:** 20 Min  🍴 **Servings:** 4

- 4 boneless, skinless chicken breasts (about 150g each)
- 120g plain Greek yogurt
- 2 tablespoons tandoori spice mix
- 1 tablespoon lemon juice
- 1 teaspoon minced garlic
- 1 teaspoon minced ginger
- 1/2 teaspoon salt
- Cooking spray or oil for greasing

# Sesame Soy Chicken Strips

🕐 **Cooking Time:** 15 Min  🍴 **Servings:** 4

- 500g boneless, skinless chicken breasts, cut into strips
- 60ml soy sauce
- 2 tablespoons honey
- 1 tablespoon sesame oil
- 1 tablespoon rice vinegar
- 2 cloves garlic, minced
- 1 teaspoon grated fresh ginger
- 1 tablespoon sesame seeds
- Cooking spray or oil for greasing

## INSTRUCTION

1. In a bowl, mix together the plain Greek yogurt, tandoori spice mix, lemon juice, minced garlic, minced ginger, and salt to make the marinade.
2. Pat the chicken breasts dry with paper towels.
3. Coat the chicken breasts with the tandoori marinade, ensuring they are evenly coated.
4. Lightly spray or brush the Zone 1 air fryer basket with cooking spray or oil to prevent sticking.
5. Place the marinated chicken breasts in Zone 1 of the Ninja Dual Zone Air Fryer, ensuring they are arranged in a single layer.
6. Select Zone 1, choose the AIR FRY program, and set the temperature to 180°C. Set the time to 20 minutes.
7. Press the START/STOP button to begin cooking.
8. After 10 minutes, carefully turn the chicken breasts over for even cooking.
9. Continue cooking for the remaining time or until the chicken breasts are cooked through and the exterior is charred in places.
10. Once done, carefully remove the chicken breasts from the air fryer and let them rest for a few minutes.
11. Serve the **Tandoori Spiced Chicken** hot with rice, naan, and your favorite chutney.

1. In a bowl, whisk together the soy sauce, honey, sesame oil, rice vinegar, minced garlic, and grated ginger to make the marinade.
2. Place the chicken strips in a shallow dish and pour the marinade over them, ensuring they are evenly coated. Let them marinate for 10-15 minutes.
3. Lightly spray or brush the Zone 1 air fryer basket with cooking spray or oil to prevent sticking.
4. Place the marinated chicken strips in Zone 1 of the Ninja Dual Zone Air Fryer, ensuring they are arranged in a single layer.
5. Select Zone 1, choose the AIR FRY program, and set the temperature to 180°C. Set the time to 15 minutes.
6. Press the START/STOP button to begin cooking.
7. After 8 minutes, carefully turn the chicken strips over for even cooking.
8. Continue cooking for the remaining time or until the chicken strips are cooked through and golden brown.
9. Once done, carefully remove the chicken strips from the air fryer and let them rest for a few minutes.
10. Sprinkle the sesame seeds over the chicken strips before serving.
11. Serve the **Sesame Soy Chicken Strips** hot with steamed rice and vegetables.

## Moroccan Spiced Turkey

🕐 **Cooking Time:** 25 Min  🍴 **Servings:** 4

- 4 turkey breast fillets (about 150g each)
- 2 tablespoons olive oil
- 2 teaspoons ground cumin
- 2 teaspoons ground coriander
- 1 teaspoon paprika
- 1 teaspoon ground cinnamon
- 1/2 teaspoon ground ginger
- 1/2 teaspoon ground turmeric
- 1/2 teaspoon salt
- 1/4 teaspoon black pepper
- Cooking spray or oil for greasing

## Crispy Herbed Chicken Tenders

🕐 **Cooking Time:** 15 Min  🍴 **Servings:** 4

- 500g chicken breast tenders
- 60g breadcrumbs
- 30g grated Parmesan cheese
- 1 teaspoon dried oregano
- 1 teaspoon dried basil
- 1/2 teaspoon garlic powder
- 1/2 teaspoon onion powder
- 1/2 teaspoon paprika
- 1/2 teaspoon salt
- 1/4 teaspoon black pepper
- 2 eggs, beaten
- Cooking spray or oil for greasing

## INSTRUCTION

1. In a small bowl, mix together the olive oil, ground cumin, ground coriander, paprika, ground cinnamon, ground ginger, ground turmeric, salt, and black pepper to make the spice rub.
2. Pat the turkey breast fillets dry with paper towels.
3. Rub the spice rub over both sides of each turkey breast fillet, ensuring they are evenly coated.
4. Lightly spray or brush the Zone 1 air fryer basket with cooking spray or oil to prevent sticking.
5. Place the spiced turkey breast fillets in Zone 1 of the Ninja Dual Zone Air Fryer, ensuring they are arranged in a single layer.
6. Select Zone 1, choose the AIR FRY program, and set the temperature to 180°C. Set the time to 25 minutes.
7. Press the START/STOP button to begin cooking.
8. After 15 minutes, carefully turn the turkey breast fillets over for even cooking.
9. Continue cooking for the remaining time or until the turkey breast fillets are cooked through and the spices are aromatic.
10. Once done, carefully remove the turkey breast fillets from the air fryer and let them rest for a few minutes.
11. Serve the **Moroccan Spiced Turkey** hot with couscous or rice and a side salad.

1. In a shallow dish, mix together the breadcrumbs, grated Parmesan cheese, dried oregano, dried basil, garlic powder, onion powder, paprika, salt, and black pepper to make the breading mixture.
2. Dip each chicken tender into the beaten eggs, then coat it with the breading mixture, pressing gently to adhere.
3. Lightly spray or brush the Zone 1 air fryer basket with cooking spray or oil to prevent sticking.
4. Place the coated chicken tenders in Zone 1 of the Ninja Dual Zone Air Fryer, ensuring they are arranged in a single layer.
5. Select Zone 1, choose the AIR FRY program, and set the temperature to 180°C. Set the time to 15 minutes.
6. Press the START/STOP button to begin cooking.
7. After 7 minutes, carefully turn the chicken tenders over for even cooking.
8. Continue cooking for the remaining time or until the chicken tenders are golden brown and crispy.
9. Once done, carefully remove the chicken tenders from the air fryer and let them rest for a few minutes.
10. Serve the **Crispy Herbed Chicken Tenders** hot with your favorite dipping sauce or side dishes.

## Chili Lime Turkey Breast

🕐 **Cooking Time:** 25 Min  🍴 **Servings:** 4

- 4 turkey breast fillets (about 150g each)
- Zest and juice of 2 limes
- 2 tablespoons olive oil
- 2 cloves garlic, minced
- 1 teaspoon chili powder
- 1/2 teaspoon cumin
- 1/2 teaspoon paprika
- 1/2 teaspoon salt
- 1/4 teaspoon black pepper
- Cooking spray or oil for greasing

## Honey Soy Chicken Drumsticks

🕐 **Cooking Time:** 25 Min  🍴 **Servings:** 4

- 8 chicken drumsticks
- 60ml soy sauce
- 60ml honey
- 2 tablespoons olive oil
- 2 cloves garlic, minced
- 1 teaspoon grated fresh ginger
- 1/2 teaspoon sesame oil
- 1/2 teaspoon Chinese five-spice powder
- 1/4 teaspoon black pepper
- Cooking spray or oil for greasing

## INSTRUCTION

1. In a bowl, whisk together the lime zest, lime juice, olive oil, minced garlic, chili powder, cumin, paprika, salt, and black pepper to make the marinade.
2. Pat the turkey breast fillets dry with paper towels.
3. Place the turkey breast fillets in a shallow dish and pour the marinade over them, ensuring they are evenly coated. Let them marinate for 15-20 minutes.
4. Lightly spray or brush the Zone 1 air fryer basket with cooking spray or oil to prevent sticking.
5. Place the marinated turkey breast fillets in Zone 1 of the Ninja Dual Zone Air Fryer, ensuring they are arranged in a single layer.
6. Select Zone 1, choose the AIR FRY program, and set the temperature to 180°C. Set the time to 25 minutes.
7. Press the START/STOP button to begin cooking.
8. After 15 minutes, carefully turn the turkey breast fillets over for even cooking.
9. Continue cooking for the remaining time or until the turkey breast fillets are cooked through and the exterior is golden and slightly crispy.
10. Once done, carefully remove the turkey breast fillets from the air fryer and let them rest for a few minutes.
11. Serve the **Chili Lime Turkey Breast** hot with rice, salad, or your favorite side dishes.

---

1. In a bowl, whisk together the soy sauce, honey, olive oil, minced garlic, grated ginger, sesame oil, Chinese five-spice powder, and black pepper to make the marinade.
2. Pat the chicken drumsticks dry with paper towels.
3. Place the chicken drumsticks in a shallow dish and pour the marinade over them, ensuring they are evenly coated. Let them marinate for 15-20 minutes.
4. Lightly spray or brush both Zone air fryer basket with cooking spray or oil to prevent sticking.
5. Evenly dividing marinated chicken drumsticks between the two zone, ensuring they are arranged in a single layer.
6. Select Zone 1, choose the AIR FRY program, and set the temperature to 180°C. Set the time to 25 minutes. Select MATCH to duplicate settings across both zones. Press the START/STOP.
7. After 15 minutes, carefully turn the chicken drumsticks over for even cooking.
8. Continue cooking for the remaining time or until the chicken drumsticks are cooked through and the exterior is golden and slightly crispy.
9. Once done, carefully remove the chicken drumsticks from the air fryer and let them rest for a few minutes.
10. Serve the **Honey Soy Chicken Drumsticks** hot with steamed rice and vegetables.

# Beef Burgers

⏱ **Cooking Time: 12 Min**   🍴 **Servings: 4**

- 500g ground beef (lean)
- 1/2 onion, finely chopped
- 1 egg
- 2 tablespoons breadcrumbs
- 1 teaspoon Worcestershire sauce
- 1/2 teaspoon garlic powder
- 1/2 teaspoon onion powder
- 1/2 teaspoon salt
- 1/4 teaspoon black pepper
- Cooking spray or oil for greasing

# Beef & Spinach Rolls

⏱ **Cooking Time: 15 Min**   🍴 **Servings: 4**

- 4 thin beef slices (such as sirloin or minute steaks)
- 60 g fresh spinach leaves
- 1/2 onion, thinly sliced
- 2 cloves garlic, minced
- 1 tablespoon olive oil
- Salt and pepper, to taste
- 1/2 teaspoon dried thyme
- Toothpicks.
- Cooking spray or oil for greasing

## INSTRUCTION

1. In a large bowl, mix together the ground beef, chopped onion, egg, breadcrumbs, Worcestershire sauce, garlic powder, onion powder, salt, and black pepper until well combined.
2. Divide the mixture into 4 equal portions and shape them into burger patties.
3. Lightly spray or brush the Zone 1 air fryer basket with cooking spray or oil to prevent sticking.
4. Place the burger patties in Zone 1 of the Ninja Dual Zone Air Fryer, ensuring they are arranged in a single layer.
5. Select Zone 1, choose the ROAST program, and set the temperature to 200°C. Set the time to 12 minutes.
6. Press the START/STOP button to begin cooking.
7. After 6 minutes, carefully flip the burger patties over for even cooking.
8. Continue cooking for the remaining time or until the burger patties are cooked through and the exterior is golden brown.
9. Once done, carefully remove the burger patties from the air fryer and let them rest for a few minutes.
10. Serve the **Beef Burgers** hot with your favorite burger toppings and buns.

1. In a skillet, heat olive oil over medium heat. Add the minced garlic and sliced onion. Sauté until the onion becomes translucent and the garlic is fragrant.
2. Add the fresh spinach leaves to the skillet and cook until wilted. Season with salt, pepper, and dried thyme. Remove from heat and let the mixture cool slightly.
3. Lay out the beef slices on a clean surface. Divide the spinach and onion mixture equally among the beef slices, spreading it evenly.
4. Roll up each beef slice tightly and secure with toothpicks to hold the rolls together.
5. Lightly spray or brush the Zone 1 air fryer basket with cooking spray or oil to prevent sticking.
6. Place the beef rolls in Zone 1. Select Zone 1, then select the AIR FRY function. Set the temperature to 200°C and the time to 12-15 minutes. Press the START/STOP button to begin cooking.
7. Flip the beef rolls halfway through the cooking time to ensure even browning.
8. Once the beef rolls are cooked and golden brown, remove them from the air fryer and let them cool slightly.
9. Serve the **beef and spinach rolls** as a delicious appetizer or main dish. Remove the toothpicks before serving.

# Beef Kebabs

🕐 **Cooking Time: 10 Min**  🍴 **Servings: 4**

- 500g beef steak (such as sirloin or rump), cut into 1-inch cubes
- 1 bell pepper, cut into chunks
- 1 red onion, cut into chunks
- 8 cherry tomatoes
- 2 tablespoons olive oil
- 2 tablespoons soy sauce
- 1 tablespoon Worcestershire sauce
- 2 cloves garlic, minced
- 1 teaspoon paprika
- 1 teaspoon ground cumin
- 1/2 teaspoon ground black pepper
- Salt to taste
- Metal or soaked wooden skewers

# Beef Meatballs

🕐 **Cooking Time: 15 Min**  🍴 **Servings: 4**

- 500g lean ground beef
- 1/2 onion, finely chopped
- 2 cloves garlic, minced
- 1 egg
- 30g breadcrumbs
- 1 tablespoon Worcestershire sauce
- 1 teaspoon dried oregano
- 1 teaspoon dried basil
- 1/2 teaspoon salt
- 1/4 teaspoon black pepper
- Cooking spray or oil for greasing

## INSTRUCTION

1. In a bowl, whisk together the olive oil, soy sauce, Worcestershire sauce, minced garlic, paprika, ground cumin, ground black pepper, and salt to make the marinade.
2. Add the beef cubes to the marinade, ensuring they are well coated. Let them marinate for 30 minutes to 1 hour in the refrigerator.
3. Thread the marinated beef cubes, bell pepper chunks, red onion chunks, and cherry tomatoes onto the skewers, alternating between ingredients.
4. Lightly spray or brush the Zone 1 with cooking spray or oil.
5. Place the assembled beef kebabs in Zone 1 of the Ninja Dual Zone Air Fryer, ensuring they are arranged in a single layer.
6. Select Zone 1, choose the ROAST program, and set the temperature to 200°C. Set the time to 10 minutes. Press the START/STOP.
7. After 5 minutes, carefully turn the kebabs over for even cooking.
8. Continue cooking for the remaining time or until the beef is cooked to your desired level of doneness and the vegetables are tender.
9. Once done, carefully remove the **beef kebabs** from the air fryer. Serve the Beef Kebabs hot with rice, salad

1. In a large bowl, combine the lean ground beef, finely chopped onion, minced garlic, egg, breadcrumbs, Worcestershire sauce, dried oregano, dried basil, salt, and black pepper. Mix until well combined.
2. Shape the mixture into meatballs, about 2 to 2.5 cm in diameter.
3. Lightly spray or brush the Zone 1 air fryer basket with cooking spray or oil to prevent sticking.
4. Place the meatballs in Zone 1 of the Ninja Dual Zone Air Fryer, ensuring they are arranged in a single layer.
5. Select Zone 1, choose the AIR FRY program, and set the temperature to 180°C. Set the time to 15 minutes.
6. Press the START/STOP button to begin cooking.
7. After 10 minutes, carefully turn the meatballs over for even cooking.
8. Continue cooking for the remaining time or until the meatballs are cooked through and browned on the outside.
9. Once done, carefully remove the meatballs from the air fryer.
10. Serve the **Beef Meatballs** hot with your favorite sauce or alongside pasta, rice, or vegetables.

# Beef Steak Bites

⏱ **Cooking Time:** 10 Min  🍴 **Servings:** 4

- 500g beef sirloin or rump steak, cut into bite-sized pieces
- 2 tablespoons olive oil
- 2 cloves garlic, minced
- 1 teaspoon smoked paprika
- 1/2 teaspoon dried thyme
- 1/2 teaspoon salt
- 1/4 teaspoon black pepper
- Cooking spray or oil for greasing

# Corned Beef Hash Patties

⏱ **Cooking Time:** 15 Min  🍴 **Servings:** 4

- 500g potatoes, peeled and diced
- 200g canned corned beef, chopped into small pieces
- 1 onion, finely chopped
- 1 teaspoon Worcestershire sauce
- Salt and pepper to taste
- Cooking spray or oil for greasing

## INSTRUCTION

1. In a bowl, mix together the olive oil, minced garlic, smoked paprika, dried thyme, salt, and black pepper.
2. Add the beef steak bites to the bowl and toss until they are evenly coated with the spice mixture.
3. Lightly spray or brush the Zone 1 air fryer basket with cooking spray or oil to prevent sticking.
4. Place the seasoned beef steak bites in Zone 1 of the Ninja Dual Zone Air Fryer, ensuring they are arranged in a single layer.
5. Select Zone 1, choose the AIR FRY program, and set the temperature to 200°C. Set the time to 10 minutes.
6. Press the START/STOP button to begin cooking.
7. After 5 minutes, carefully shake the basket or turn the steak bites for even cooking.
8. Continue cooking for the remaining time or until the steak bites are cooked to your desired level of doneness and are browned on the outside.
9. Once done, carefully remove the beef steak bites from the air fryer.
10. Serve the **Beef Steak Bites** hot as an appetizer or main dish.

1. Place the diced potatoes in a saucepan and cover with cold water. Bring to a boil, then reduce the heat and simmer for about 10 minutes or until the potatoes are tender. Drain and set aside to cool slightly.
2. In a large bowl, combine the cooked potatoes, chopped corned beef, finely chopped onion, Worcestershire sauce, salt, and pepper. Mix well to combine.
3. Shape the potato mixture into patties, about 1.5-2 cm thick.
4. Lightly spray or brush the Zone 1 air fryer basket with cooking spray or oil to prevent sticking.
5. Place the patties in Zone 1 of the Ninja Dual Zone Air Fryer, ensuring they are arranged in a single layer.
6. Select Zone 1, choose the AIR FRY program, and set the temperature to 180°C. Set the time to 15 minutes. Press the START/STOP.
7. After 7-8 minutes, carefully flip the patties over for even cooking.
8. Continue cooking for the remaining time or until the patties are golden brown and crispy on the outside.
9. Once done, carefully remove the corned beef hash patties from the air fryer.
10. Serve the **Corned Beef Hash Patties** hot with eggs, toast, or your favorite breakfast sides.

# Beef & Lamb Gyros

🕐 Cooking Time: 20 Min  🍴 Servings: 4

- 250g ground beef
- 250g ground lamb
- 1 onion, grated
- 2 cloves garlic, minced
- 1 teaspoon dried oregano
- 1 teaspoon ground cumin
- 1 teaspoon paprika
- 1/2 teaspoon ground coriander
- Salt and pepper to taste
- Cooking spray or oil for greasing (optional)
- Pita bread, to serve
- Tzatziki sauce, to serve
- Chopped tomatoes, lettuce, and onions, to serve

# Beef Teriyaki Skewers

🕐 Cooking Time: 15 Min  🍴 Servings: 4

- 500g beef steak, cut into cubes
- 60ml soy sauce
- 30ml mirin
- 30ml sake (or dry sherry)
- 30g brown sugar
- 2 cloves garlic, minced
- 1 teaspoon grated fresh ginger
- Cooking spray or oil for greasing (optional)
- Wooden or metal skewers

## INSTRUCTION

1. In a bowl, combine the ground beef, ground lamb, grated onion, minced garlic, dried oregano, ground cumin, paprika, ground coriander, salt, and pepper. Mix well to combine.
2. If desired, lightly spray or brush the air fryer basket with cooking spray or oil to prevent sticking.
3. Divide the meat mixture into 4 equal portions and shape each portion into a log shape.
4. Place the meat logs in Zone 1 of the Ninja Dual Zone Air Fryer, ensuring they are arranged in a single layer.
5. Select Zone 1, choose the AIR FRY program, and set the temperature to 200°C. Set the time to 20 minutes. Press the START/STOP.
6. After 10 minutes, carefully turn the meat logs over for even cooking.
7. Continue cooking for the remaining time or until the meat is cooked through and browned on the outside.
8. Once done, carefully remove the meat logs from the air fryer.
9. Warm the pita bread in the air fryer for a few minutes if desired. Serve the **Beef & Lamb Gyros** by slicing the meat and placing it on the warm pita bread. Top with tzatziki sauce, chopped tomatoes, lettuce, and onions.

1. In a bowl, mix together the soy sauce, mirin, sake, brown sugar, minced garlic, and grated ginger to make the teriyaki marinade.
2. Add the beef cubes to the marinade, making sure they are well coated. Let them marinate for at least 30 minutes in the refrigerator.
3. If using wooden skewers, soak them in water for at least 30 minutes to prevent burning.
4. Thread the marinated beef cubes onto the skewers.
5. Place the beef skewers in Zone 1 of the Ninja Dual Zone Air Fryer, ensuring they are arranged in a single layer.
6. Select Zone 1, choose the AIR FRY program, and set the temperature to 200°C. Set the time to 15 minutes.
7. Press the START/STOP button to begin cooking.
8. After 8-10 minutes, carefully turn the skewers over for even cooking.
9. Continue cooking for the remaining time or until the beef is cooked to your desired level of doneness and has a nice caramelized exterior.
10. Once done, carefully remove the beef teriyaki skewers from the air fryer.
11. Serve the **Beef Teriyaki Skewers** hot with steamed rice and vegetables.

## Beef Satay Skewers

🕐 **Cooking Time:** 15 Min  🍴 **Servings:** 4

- 500g beef steak (such as sirloin or rump), thinly sliced
- 2 tablespoons soy sauce
- 2 tablespoons coconut milk
- 1 tablespoon brown sugar
- 1 tablespoon vegetable oil
- 1 clove garlic, minced
- 1 teaspoon ground coriander
- 1 teaspoon ground cumin
- 1/2 teaspoon turmeric
- 1/2 teaspoon chili powder (adjust to taste)
- Wooden or metal skewers

## BBQ Beef Ribs

🕐 **Cooking Time:** 30 Min  🍴 **Servings:** 4

- 1 kg beef ribs, cut into individual pieces
- Salt and pepper to taste
- 1 cup BBQ sauce
- 2 tablespoons Worcestershire sauce
- 1 tablespoon brown sugar
- 1 tablespoon apple cider vinegar
- 1 teaspoon smoked paprika
- 1/2 teaspoon garlic powder
- Cooking spray or oil for greasing (optional)

## INSTRUCTION

1. In a bowl, mix together the soy sauce, coconut milk, brown sugar, vegetable oil, minced garlic, ground coriander, ground cumin, turmeric, and chili powder to make the marinade.
2. Add the thinly sliced beef to the marinade, making sure it is well coated. Let it marinate for at least 30 minutes in the refrigerator.
3. If using wooden skewers, soak them in water for at least 30 minutes to prevent burning.
4. Thread the marinated beef slices onto the skewers.
5. Place the beef satay skewers in Zone 1 of the Ninja Dual Zone Air Fryer, ensuring they are arranged in a single layer.
6. Select Zone 1, choose the AIR FRY program, and set the temperature to 200°C. Set the time to 15 minutes. Press the START/STOP.
7. After 8-10 minutes, carefully turn the skewers over for even cooking.
8. Continue cooking for the remaining time or until the beef is cooked through and has a nice charred exterior.
9. Once done, carefully remove the beef satay skewers from the air fryer.
10. Serve the **Beef Satay Skewers** hot with peanut sauce and a side of cucumber salad or rice.

1. Season the beef ribs with salt and pepper.
2. In a bowl, mix together the BBQ sauce, Worcestershire sauce, brown sugar, apple cider vinegar, smoked paprika, and garlic powder to make the BBQ marinade.
3. Coat the beef ribs with the BBQ marinade, ensuring they are well coated on all sides.
4. Evenly dividing beef ribs between the two zone, ensuring they are in a single layer.
5. Select Zone 1, choose the AIR FRY program, and set the temperature to 180°C. Set the time to 25-30 minutes. Select MATCH to duplicate settings across both zones. Press the START/STOP.
6. After 15 minutes, carefully turn the beef ribs over for even cooking.
7. Continue cooking for the remaining time or until the beef ribs are tender and the BBQ sauce has caramelized.
8. Once done, carefully remove the beef ribs from the air fryer.
9. Serve the **BBQ Beef Ribs** hot with your favorite sides, such as coleslaw, cornbread, or baked beans.

# Beef Fajitas

🕐 **Cooking Time:** 15 Min  🍽 **Servings:** 4

- 500g beef steak (such as sirloin or flank), thinly sliced
- 1 onion, sliced
- 1 bell pepper (any color), sliced
- 2 tablespoons olive oil
- 1 tablespoon lime juice
- 1 teaspoon chili powder
- 1 teaspoon ground cumin
- 1/2 teaspoon smoked paprika
- 1/2 teaspoon garlic powder
- Salt and pepper to taste
- Flour tortillas, for serving
- Optional toppings: salsa, guacamole, sour cream, shredded cheese, chopped cilantro

# Pork Tenderloin

🕐 **Cooking Time:** 20 Min  🍽 **Servings:** 4

- 500g pork tenderloin
- 1 tablespoon olive oil
- 2 cloves garlic, minced
- 1 teaspoon dried thyme
- 1 teaspoon dried rosemary
- 1/2 teaspoon paprika
- Salt and pepper to taste

## INSTRUCTION

**Beef Fajitas**

1. In a bowl, combine the sliced beef steak, sliced onion, sliced bell pepper, olive oil, lime juice, chili powder, ground cumin, smoked paprika, garlic powder, salt, and pepper. Toss to coat the beef and vegetables evenly with the marinade.
2. If desired, lightly spray or brush the Zone 1 air fryer basket with cooking spray or oil to prevent sticking.
3. Place the marinated beef and vegetables in Zone 1 of the Ninja Dual Zone Air Fryer, ensuring they are arranged in a single layer.
4. Select Zone 1, choose the AIR FRY program, and set the temperature to 200°C. Set the time to 15 minutes. Press the START/STOP.
5. After 8-10 minutes, carefully toss the beef and vegetables to ensure even cooking.
6. Continue cooking for the remaining time or until the beef is cooked through and the vegetables are tender and slightly charred.
7. Once done, carefully remove the beef fajita mixture from the air fryer.
8. Serve the **Beef Fajitas** with warm flour tortillas and optional toppings such as salsa, guacamole, sour cream, shredded cheese, and chopped cilantro.

**Pork Tenderloin**

1. In a small bowl, mix together the olive oil, minced garlic, dried thyme, dried rosemary, paprika, salt, and pepper to create a marinade.
2. Rub the pork tenderloin with the marinade, ensuring it is evenly coated.
3. Place the pork tenderloin in Zone 1 of the Ninja Dual Zone Air Fryer.
4. Select Zone 1, choose the ROAST program, and set the temperature to 180°C. Set the time to 20 minutes.
5. Press the START/STOP button to begin cooking.
6. After 10 minutes, carefully turn the pork tenderloin for even cooking.
7. Continue cooking for the remaining time or until the pork is cooked through and reaches an internal temperature of 63°C.
8. Once done, carefully remove the pork tenderloin from the air fryer and let it rest for a few minutes before slicing.
9. Serve the **Pork Tenderloin** hot with your favorite sides, such as roasted vegetables or mashed potatoes.

# Pulled Pork Sliders

⏱ **Cooking Time:** 30 Min   🍴 **Servings:** 4-6

- 500g pork shoulder or pork butt, trimmed of excess fat
- 1 tablespoon olive oil
- 1 onion, finely chopped
- 2 cloves garlic, minced
- 240ml barbecue sauce
- 120ml chicken or vegetable broth
- 1 teaspoon smoked paprika
- 1 teaspoon ground cumin
- 1 teaspoon brown sugar
- Salt and pepper to taste
- Slider buns
- Coleslaw (optional, for serving)

# Pork Sausages

⏱ **Cooking Time:** 20 Min   🍴 **Servings:** 4

- 8 pork sausages
- Cooking spray or oil for greasing (optional)

## INSTRUCTION

1. Cut the pork shoulder or pork butt into large chunks.
2. In a large bowl, mix together the olive oil, chopped onion, minced garlic, barbecue sauce, chicken or vegetable broth, smoked paprika, ground cumin, brown sugar, salt, and pepper.
3. Add the pork chunks to the bowl and toss until they are well coated with the sauce mixture.
4. Transfer the coated pork chunks to Zone 1 of the air fryer, ensuring they are in a single layer.
5. Select Zone 1, choose the ROAST program, and set the temperature to 160°C. Set the time to 30 minutes.
6. Press the START/STOP button to begin cooking.
7. After 15 minutes, carefully turn the pork chunks over for even cooking.
8. Continue cooking for the remaining time or until the pork is tender and easily pulls apart with a fork.
9. Once done, carefully remove the pork from the air fryer and use two forks to shred it.
10. Serve the **pulled pork** on slider buns with coleslaw if desired.

1. If desired, lightly spray or brush the air fryer basket with cooking spray or oil to prevent sticking.
2. Place the pork sausages in Zone 1 of the Ninja Dual Zone Air Fryer, ensuring they are arranged in a single layer.
3. Select Zone 1, choose the AIR FRY program, and set the temperature to 200°C. Set the time to 15-20 minutes, depending on the thickness of the sausages and your desired level of doneness.
4. Press the START/STOP button to begin cooking.
5. After 10 minutes, carefully turn the sausages over for even cooking.
6. Continue cooking for the remaining time or until the sausages are cooked through and browned on the outside.
7. Once done, carefully remove the pork sausages from the air fryer.
8. Serve the **Pork Sausages** hot with your favorite sides, such as mashed potatoes and gravy, or in a bun as a hot dog.

# Pork Belly Bites

🕒 **Cooking Time:** 40 Min   🍴 **Servings:** 4

- 500g pork belly, skin removed and cut into bite-sized pieces
- 1 tablespoon soy sauce
- 1 tablespoon hoisin sauce
- 1 tablespoon honey
- 1 teaspoon five-spice powder
- 1 teaspoon garlic powder
- 1/2 teaspoon ground ginger
- 1/2 teaspoon salt
- Cooking spray or oil for greasing (optional)

# Pork Schnitzel Bites

🕒 **Cooking Time:** 15 Min   🍴 **Servings:** 4

- 500g pork loin or tenderloin, thinly sliced into bite-sized pieces
- 2 eggs, beaten
- 100g breadcrumbs
- 50g all-purpose flour
- 1 teaspoon paprika
- 1 teaspoon garlic powder
- Salt and pepper to taste
- Cooking spray or oil for greasing (optional)
- Lemon wedges, for serving
- Fresh parsley, chopped, for garnish

## INSTRUCTION

1. In a bowl, mix together the soy sauce, hoisin sauce, honey, five-spice powder, garlic powder, ground ginger, and salt to create a marinade.
2. Add the pork belly pieces to the marinade, ensuring they are well coated. Let them marinate for at least 30 minutes in the refrigerator.
3. Preheat the Ninja Dual Zone Air Fryer to 180°C.
4. If desired, lightly spray or brush the Zone 1 air fryer basket with cooking spray or oil to prevent sticking.
5. Place the marinated pork belly pieces in Zone 1 of the Ninja Dual Zone Air Fryer, ensuring they are arranged in a single layer.
6. Select Zone 1, choose the AIR FRY program, and set the temperature to 180°C. Set the time to 30-40 minutes, depending on the size and thickness of the pork belly pieces.
7. Press the START/STOP button to begin cooking.
8. Turn them halfway through cooking for even browning.
9. Once done, carefully remove the pork belly bites from the air fryer.
10. Serve the **Pork Belly Bites** hot as a delicious appetizer or main dish.

1. In a shallow dish, mix together the breadcrumbs, all-purpose flour, paprika, garlic powder, salt, and pepper.
2. Dip each piece of pork into the beaten eggs, then coat with the breadcrumb mixture, pressing gently to adhere.
3. If desired, lightly spray or brush the Zone 1 air fryer basket with cooking spray or oil to prevent sticking.
4. Place the breaded pork schnitzel bites in Zone 1 of the Ninja Dual Zone Air Fryer, ensuring they are arranged in a single layer.
5. Select Zone 1, choose the AIR FRY program, and set the temperature to 200°C. Set the time to 15 minutes.
6. Press the START/STOP button to begin cooking.
7. After 8-10 minutes, carefully turn the pork schnitzel bites over for even cooking.
8. Continue cooking for the remaining time or until the pork is golden brown and cooked through.
9. Once done, carefully remove the pork schnitzel bites from the air fryer.
10. Serve the **Pork Schnitzel Bites** hot with lemon wedges for squeezing and garnish with chopped fresh parsley.

# Crispy Pork Carnitas

🕐 **Cooking Time:** 25 Min  🍴 **Servings:** 4

- 1 kg pork shoulder, cut into chunks
- 1 onion, quartered
- 4 cloves garlic, crushed
- 1 teaspoon ground cumin
- 1 teaspoon dried oregano
- 1 teaspoon smoked paprika
- 1 teaspoon salt
- 1/2 teaspoon black pepper
- 120ml orange juice
- 30ml lime juice
- Cooking spray or oil for greasing (optional)

# Pork Stir-Fried Rice

🕐 **Cooking Time:** 20 Min  🍴 **Servings:** 4

- 300g pork tenderloin, thinly sliced
- 450g cooked rice, preferably chilled
- 2 eggs, beaten
- 150g mixed vegetables (such as peas, carrots, and corn)
- 2 spring onions, chopped
- 2 cloves garlic, minced
- 30ml soy sauce
- 15ml oyster sauce
- 15ml vegetable oil
- Salt and pepper to taste
- Cooking spray or oil for greasing (optional)

## INSTRUCTION

**Crispy Pork Carnitas:**

1. Place the pork chunks, onion quarters, crushed garlic, ground cumin, dried oregano, smoked paprika, salt, and black pepper in a bowl. Mix well to coat the pork with the seasonings.
2. If desired, lightly spray or brush the both air fryer basket with cooking spray or oil to prevent sticking.
3. Place the seasoned pork mixture in two Zone of the Ninja Dual Zone Air Fryer, ensuring it is spread out in a single layer.
4. Select Zone 1, choose the AIR FRY program, and set the temperature to 180°C. Set the time to 25 minutes. Select MATCH to duplicate settings across both zones. Press the START/STOP.
5. After 15 minutes, carefully toss the pork to ensure even cooking.
6. Continue cooking for the remaining time or until the pork is tender and crispy on the outside.
7. Once done, carefully remove the crispy pork carnitas from the air fryer.
8. Serve the **Crispy Pork Carnitas** hot with tortillas, salsa, guacamole, and your favorite toppings.

**Pork Stir-Fried Rice:**

1. Preheat the Ninja Dual Zone Air Fryer to 180°C using the AIR FRY setting.
2. If using raw rice, cook it according to package instructions and chill it beforehand for best results.
3. In Zone 1 of the air fryer, heat the vegetable oil using the AIR FRY setting.
4. Add the minced garlic and stir-fry for about 30 seconds until fragrant.
5. Add the thinly sliced pork tenderloin to Zone 1 and stir-fry until cooked through.
6. Push the cooked pork to one side of Zone 1, then add the beaten eggs to the other side. Scramble the eggs until cooked, then mix them with the pork.
7. Add the mixed vegetables to Zone 1 and stir-fry for a few minutes until they are heated through.
8. Add the chilled cooked rice to Zone 1, breaking up any clumps, and stir-fry everything together for a few minutes.
9. Drizzle the soy sauce and oyster sauce over the rice mixture in Zone 1 and continue to stir-fry for another 2-3 minutes, ensuring everything is well combined.
10. Season with salt and pepper to taste.
11. Once done, carefully remove the Pork Stir-Fried Rice from the air fryer. Serve the **Pork Stir-Fried Rice** hot, garnished with chopped spring onions.

# Lamb Chops

🕐 **Cooking Time: 20 Min**  🍴 **Servings: 4**

- 8 lamb chops
- 2 tablespoons olive oil
- 2 cloves garlic, minced
- 1 teaspoon dried rosemary
- 1 teaspoon dried thyme
- Salt and pepper to taste
- Cooking spray or oil for greasing (optional)

# Lamb Kofta

🕐 **Cooking Time: 15 Min**  🍴 **Servings: 4**

- 500g ground lamb
- 1 onion, finely chopped
- 2 cloves garlic, minced
- 1 teaspoon ground cumin
- 1 teaspoon ground coriander
- 1 teaspoon paprika
- 1/2 teaspoon ground cinnamon
- 1/4 teaspoon cayenne pepper (optional, adjust to taste)
- Salt and pepper to taste
- Cooking spray or oil for greasing (optional)

## INSTRUCTION

1. In a small bowl, mix together the olive oil, minced garlic, dried rosemary, dried thyme, salt, and pepper.
2. Rub the lamb chops with the seasoned oil mixture, ensuring they are well coated.
3. If desired, lightly spray or brush the air fryer basket with cooking spray or oil to prevent sticking.
4. Evenly dividing lamb chops between the two zone, ensuring they are arranged in a single layer.
5. Select Zone 1, choose the AIR FRY program, and set the temperature to 200°C. Set the time to 15-20 minutes, depending on the thickness of the lamb chops and your desired level of doneness.
6. Select MATCH to duplicate settings across both zones. Press the START/STOP button to begin cooking.
7. After 10 minutes, carefully turn the lamb chops over for even cooking.
8. Continue cooking for the remaining time or until the lamb chops are cooked to your desired level of doneness and are browned on the outside.
9. Once done, carefully remove the lamb chops from the air fryer.
10. Serve the **Lamb Chops** hot with your favorite sides, such as roasted vegetables or couscous.

1. In a large bowl, combine the ground lamb, finely chopped onion, minced garlic, ground cumin, ground coriander, paprika, ground cinnamon, cayenne pepper (if using), salt, and pepper. Mix until well combined.
2. Divide the lamb mixture into equal portions and shape each portion into a cylindrical kofta shape.
3. If desired, lightly spray or brush the Zone 1 basket with cooking spray or oil to prevent sticking.
4. Place the lamb koftas in Zone 1 of the Ninja Dual Zone Air Fryer, ensuring they are arranged in a single layer.
5. Select Zone 1, choose the AIR FRY program, and set the temperature to 180°C. Set the time to 15 minutes.
6. Press the START/STOP button to begin cooking.
7. After 7-8 minutes, carefully turn the koftas over for even cooking.
8. Continue cooking for the remaining time or until the lamb koftas are cooked through and browned on the outside.
9. Once done, carefully remove the lamb koftas from the air fryer.
10. Serve the **Lamb Kofta** hot with pita bread, salad, and a yogurt-based sauce.

# Lamb Shawarma

⏱ Cooking Time: 20 Min   🍴 Servings: 4

- 500g boneless lamb leg or shoulder, thinly sliced
- 2 tablespoons olive oil
- 2 cloves garlic, minced
- 1 teaspoon ground cumin
- 1 teaspoon ground coriander
- 1 teaspoon paprika
- 1/2 teaspoon ground cinnamon
- 1/2 teaspoon ground turmeric
- 1/4 teaspoon cayenne pepper (adjust to taste)
- Salt and pepper to taste
- Cooking spray or oil for greasing (optional)

# Lamb Skewers

⏱ Cooking Time: 15 Min   🍴 Servings: 4

- 500g lamb leg or shoulder, cut into cubes
- 1 onion, cut into chunks
- 1 bell pepper, cut into chunks
- 2 tablespoons olive oil
- 2 cloves garlic, minced
- 1 teaspoon dried oregano
- 1 teaspoon dried thyme
- 1 teaspoon paprika
- Salt and pepper to taste
- Wooden or metal skewers
- Cooking spray or oil for greasing (optional)

## INSTRUCTION

1. In a bowl, combine the olive oil, minced garlic, ground cumin, ground coriander, paprika, ground cinnamon, ground turmeric, cayenne pepper, salt, and pepper to create a marinade.
2. Add the thinly sliced lamb to the marinade, ensuring it is well coated. Let it marinate for at least 30 minutes in the refrigerator.
3. If desired, lightly spray or brush the Zone 1 air fryer basket with cooking spray or oil to prevent sticking.
4. Place the marinated lamb slices in Zone 1 of the Ninja Dual Zone Air Fryer, ensuring they are arranged in a single layer.
5. Select Zone 1, choose the AIR FRY program, and set the temperature to 180°C. Set the time to 20 minutes.
6. Press the START/STOP button to begin cooking.
7. After 10 minutes, carefully turn the lamb slices over for even cooking.
8. Continue cooking for the remaining time or until the lamb is cooked through and slightly crispy on the edges.
9. Once done, carefully remove the lamb from the air fryer.
10. Serve the **Lamb Shawarma** hot with pita bread, salad, and a yogurt-based sauce.

1. If using wooden skewers, soak them in water for at least 30 minutes to prevent burning.
2. In a bowl, mix together the olive oil, minced garlic, dried oregano, dried thyme, paprika, salt, and pepper.
3. Add the lamb cubes to the bowl and toss until they are well coated with the marinade. Let them marinate for at least 30 minutes in the refrigerator.
4. If using wooden skewers, thread the marinated lamb cubes onto the skewers, alternating with chunks of onion and bell pepper.
5. Lightly spray or brush the Zone 1 basket with cooking spray or oil to prevent sticking.
6. Place the assembled skewers in Zone 1 of the Ninja Dual Zone Air Fryer, ensuring they are arranged in a single layer.
7. Select Zone 1, choose the AIR FRY program, and set the temperature to 200°C. Set the time to 15 minutes. Press the START/STOP.
8. After 7-8 minutes, carefully turn the skewers over for even cooking.
9. Continue cooking for the remaining time or until the lamb is cooked through and the vegetables are tender.
10. Once done, carefully remove the skewers from the air fryer. Serve the **Lamb Skewers** hot with rice, salad, or pita bread.

# Lamb Meatballs

🕐 **Cooking Time: 15 Min**   🍴 **Servings: 4**

- 500g ground lamb
- 1/2 onion, finely chopped
- 2 cloves garlic, minced
- 25 g breadcrumbs
- 1 egg
- 2 tablespoons chopped fresh parsley
- 1 teaspoon ground cumin
- 1 teaspoon ground coriander
- 1/2 teaspoon paprika
- Salt and pepper to taste
- Cooking spray or oil for greasing (optional)

# Mixed Grill Platter

🕐 **Cooking Time: 25 Min**   🍴 **Servings: 4**

- 4 lamb chops
- 4 pork sausages
- 4 chicken skewers (chicken breast or thigh meat, cut into chunks and threaded onto skewers)
- 1 onion, cut into chunks
- 1 bell pepper, cut into chunks
- 2 tablespoons olive oil
- 2 cloves garlic, minced
- 1 teaspoon dried oregano
- 1 teaspoon dried thyme
- 1 teaspoon paprika
- Salt and pepper to taste
- Wooden or metal skewers
- Cooking spray or oil for greasing (optional)

## INSTRUCTION

1. In a large bowl, combine the ground lamb, finely chopped onion, minced garlic, breadcrumbs, egg, chopped fresh parsley, ground cumin, ground coriander, paprika, salt, and pepper. Mix until well combined.
2. Shape the lamb mixture into meatballs, about 2.5 to 3 cm in diameter.
3. If desired, lightly spray or brush the Zone 1 air fryer basket with cooking spray or oil to prevent sticking.
4. Place the meatballs in Zone 1 of the Ninja Dual Zone Air Fryer, ensuring they are arranged in a single layer.
5. Select Zone 1, choose the AIR FRY program, and set the temperature to 180°C. Set the time to 15 minutes.
6. Press the START/STOP button to begin cooking.
7. After 10 minutes, carefully turn the meatballs over for even cooking.
8. Continue cooking for the remaining time or until the meatballs are browned and cooked through.
9. Once done, carefully remove the meatballs from the air fryer.
10. Serve the **Lamb Meatballs** hot with your favorite sauce, pasta, or salad.

---

1. If using wooden skewers, soak them in water for at least 30 minutes to prevent burning.
2. In a bowl, mix together the olive oil, minced garlic, dried oregano, dried thyme, paprika, salt, and pepper.
3. Divide the marinade into two portions. Use one portion to coat the lamb chops and the other portion to coat the chicken skewers.
4. Evenly dividing marinated lamb chops, pork sausages, chicken skewers, onion chunks, and bell pepper chunks between the two zone, ensuring they are arranged in a single layer.
5. Select Zone 1, choose the AIR FRY program, and set the temperature to 200°C. Set the time to 20-25 minutes. Select MATCH to duplicate settings across both zones. Press the START/STOP.
6. After 10 minutes, carefully turn the meat and vegetables for even cooking.
7. Continue cooking for the remaining time or until the meats are cooked through and the vegetables are tender.
8. Once done, carefully remove the mixed grill platter from the air fryer.
9. Serve the **Mixed Grill Platter** hot with your favorite sides, such as rice, salad, or grilled bread.

## Sausage Rolls

🕐 **Cooking Time:** 20 Min  🍴 **Servings:** 4

- 500g sausage meat or sausage filling (removed from casings if using sausages)
- 1 sheet of ready-rolled puff pastry
- 1 egg, beaten (for egg wash)
- Sesame seeds or poppy seeds (optional, for topping)
- Cooking spray or oil for greasing (optional)

## Meat Pies

🕐 **Cooking Time:** 20 Min  🍴 **Servings:** 4

- 500g ground beef or lamb
- 1 onion, finely chopped
- 2 cloves garlic, minced
- 1 carrot, finely diced
- 1 celery stalk, finely diced
- 80 g frozen peas
- 2 tablespoons tomato paste
- 1 teaspoon Worcestershire sauce
- 1 teaspoon dried thyme
- 1 teaspoon dried rosemary
- Salt and pepper to taste
- 1 sheet of ready-rolled puff pastry
- 1 egg, beaten (for egg wash)

---

## INSTRUCTION

---

1. If using sausage meat, divide it into 4 equal portions.
2. Cut the puff pastry sheet into 4 equal rectangles.
3. Place a portion of sausage meat along the length of each puff pastry rectangle.
4. Roll up the pastry around the sausage meat, sealing the edges with a little water. Trim any excess pastry if needed.
5. If desired, lightly spray or brush the Zone 1 air fryer basket with cooking spray or oil to prevent sticking.
6. Place the sausage rolls in Zone 1 of the Ninja Dual Zone Air Fryer, ensuring they are arranged seam-side down in a single layer.
7. Brush the tops of the sausage rolls with beaten egg and sprinkle with sesame seeds or poppy seeds if using.
8. Select Zone 1, choose the AIR FRY program, and set the temperature to 180°C. Set the time to 15-20 minutes. Press the START/STOP.
9. Check the sausage rolls after 10 minutes to ensure they are cooking evenly. If needed, rotate them for even browning.
10. Continue cooking for the remaining time or until the sausage rolls are golden brown and cooked through.
11. Once done, carefully remove the sausage rolls from the air fryer. Serve the **Sausage Rolls** hot as a snack or with a side salad for a meal.

1. In a pan, brown the ground beef or lamb over medium heat. Add the onion, garlic, carrot, and celery, and cook until the vegetables are softened.
2. Stir in the frozen peas, tomato paste, Worcestershire sauce, dried thyme, dried rosemary, salt, and pepper. Cook for another 2-3 minutes, then remove from heat and let the mixture cool slightly.
3. Cut the puff pastry sheet into 4 equal squares.
4. Place a portion of the meat mixture onto each square of puff pastry.
5. Fold the pastry over the filling to form a triangle or rectangle shape. Press the edges to seal, and crimp with a fork if desired.
6. Place the meat pies in Zone 1, ensuring they are arranged in a single layer.
7. Brush the tops of the meat pies with beaten egg.
8. Select Zone 1, choose the AIR FRY program, and set the temperature to 180°C. Set the time to 15-20 minutes. Press the START/STOP.
9. Check the meat pies after 10 minutes to ensure they are cooking evenly. If needed, rotate them for even browning.
10. Continue cooking for the remaining time or until the meat pies are golden brown and cooked through.
11. Once done, carefully remove the **meat pies** from the air fryer. Serve the Meat Pies hot.

# Miso Glazed Black Cod

🕐 **Cooking Time: 8 Min**  🍴 **Servings: 4**

- 4 black cod fillets (about 150g each)
- 60g white miso paste
- 30g mirin
- 30g sake (or dry sherry)
- 15g sugar
- 15g vegetable oil
- 1 tablespoon water
- Sesame seeds and chopped spring onions for garnish

# Fish Tacos

🕐 **Cooking Time: 10 Min**  🍴 **Servings: 4**

- 500g firm white fish fillets (such as cod or haddock), cut into strips
- 1 teaspoon smoked paprika
- 1 teaspoon ground cumin
- 1/2 teaspoon garlic powder
- 1/2 teaspoon onion powder
- 1/2 teaspoon chili powder
- 1/2 teaspoon salt
- 1/4 teaspoon black pepper
- 1 tablespoon olive oil
- 8 small corn tortillas
- Shredded cabbage or lettuce
- Diced tomatoes
- Sliced avocado
- Lime wedges
- Fresh cilantro leaves
- Hot sauce (optional)

---

## INSTRUCTION

---

1. In a bowl, mix together the white miso paste, mirin, sake, sugar, vegetable oil, and water to create the miso glaze.
2. Place the black cod fillets in a shallow dish and coat them evenly with the miso glaze. Marinate the fillets in the refrigerator for at least 30 minutes.
3. If desired, lightly spray or brush the Zone 1 air fryer basket with cooking spray or oil to prevent sticking.
4. Place the marinated black cod fillets in Zone 1 of the Ninja Dual Zone Air Fryer, ensuring they are arranged in a single layer.
5. Select Zone 1, choose the AIR FRY program, and set the temperature to 180°C. Set the time to 12-15 minutes.
6. Press the START/STOP button to begin cooking.
7. After 8-10 minutes, carefully check the black cod fillets for doneness. They should be opaque and flake easily with a fork.
8. Once done, carefully remove the miso glazed black cod fillets from the air fryer.
9. Garnish with sesame seeds and chopped spring onions.
10. Serve the **Miso Glazed Black Cod** hot, accompanied by steamed rice and vegetables.

1. In a bowl, combine the smoked paprika, ground cumin, garlic powder, onion powder, chili powder, salt, pepper, and olive oil to make a spice rub.
2. Pat the fish fillets dry with paper towels, then rub the spice mixture evenly over the fish.
3. Place the fish fillets in Zone 1 of the Ninja Dual Zone Air Fryer, ensuring they are arranged in a single layer.
4. Select Zone 1, choose the AIR FRY program, and set the temperature to 200°C. Set the time to 10 minutes.
5. Press the START/STOP button to begin cooking.
6. While the fish is cooking, warm the corn tortillas in a dry skillet over medium heat or in the microwave.
7. Once the fish is done, remove it from the air fryer.
8. Assemble the fish tacos by placing some shredded cabbage or lettuce on each tortilla, followed by a few pieces of the cooked fish.
9. Top with diced tomatoes, sliced avocado, a squeeze of lime juice, fresh cilantro leaves, and hot sauce if desired.
10. Serve the **Fish Tacos** immediately, with extra lime wedges on the side

# Prawn Tempura

⏱ **Cooking Time:** 10 Min  🍴 **Servings:** 4

- 300g large prawns, peeled and deveined
- 100g plain flour
- 50g cornflour
- 1/2 teaspoon baking powder
- 1/2 teaspoon salt
- 1 egg, beaten
- 200ml ice-cold water
- Cooking spray or oil for greasing (optional)
- Tempura dipping sauce (store-bought or homemade)

# Salmon Patties

⏱ **Cooking Time:** 12 Min  🍴 **Servings:** 4

- 450g canned salmon, drained and flaked
- 75g breadcrumbs
- 1 small onion, finely chopped
- 1 small celery stalk, finely chopped
- 1 small red bell pepper, finely chopped
- 1 egg, beaten
- 30g mayonnaise
- 15g Dijon mustard
- 15ml lemon juice
- 5ml Old Bay seasoning (optional)
- Salt and pepper to taste
- Cooking spray or oil for greasing (optional)

## INSTRUCTION

1. In a bowl, combine the plain flour, cornflour, baking powder, and salt.
2. In another bowl, whisk together the beaten egg and ice-cold water.
3. Gradually add the wet ingredients to the dry ingredients, whisking until just combined. Be careful not to overmix; it's okay if the batter is slightly lumpy.
4. Dip the prawns into the batter, coating them evenly.
5. If desired, lightly spray or brush the Zone 1 air fryer basket with cooking spray or oil to prevent sticking.
6. Place the battered prawns in Zone 1 of the Ninja Dual Zone Air Fryer, ensuring they are arranged in a single layer.
7. Select Zone 1, choose the AIR FRY program, and set the temperature to 200°C. Set the time to 8-10 minutes.
8. Press the START/STOP button to begin cooking.
9. After 4-5 minutes, carefully turn the prawns over for even cooking.
10. Continue cooking for the remaining time or until the prawns are golden brown and crispy.
11. Once done, carefully remove the prawn tempura from the air fryer.
12. Serve the **Prawn Tempura** hot with tempura dipping sauce on the side.

1. In a large bowl, combine the flaked salmon, breadcrumbs, chopped onion, chopped celery, chopped red bell pepper, beaten egg, mayonnaise, Dijon mustard, lemon juice, Old Bay seasoning (if using), salt, and pepper. Mix well until all ingredients are combined.
2. Form the mixture into 8 patties, each about 1/2 inch thick.
3. If desired, lightly spray or brush the Zone 1 air fryer basket with cooking spray or oil to prevent sticking.
4. Place the salmon patties in Zone 1 of the Ninja Dual Zone Air Fryer, ensuring they are arranged in a single layer.
5. Select Zone 1, choose the AIR FRY program, and set the temperature to 180°C. Set the time to 10-12 minutes.
6. Press the START/STOP button to begin cooking.
7. After 5-6 minutes, carefully flip the salmon patties over for even cooking.
8. Continue cooking for the remaining time or until the salmon patties are golden brown and crispy.
9. Once done, carefully remove the salmon patties from the air fryer.
10. Serve the **Salmon Patties** hot with a side of tartar sauce or your favorite dipping sauce.

# Scampi

🕐 Cooking Time: 10 Min  🍴 Servings: 4

- 400g raw scampi tails, peeled and deveined
- 100g plain flour
- 2 eggs, beaten
- 100g breadcrumbs
- 1 teaspoon garlic powder
- 1 teaspoon paprika
- 1/2 teaspoon salt
- 1/2 teaspoon black pepper
- Cooking spray or oil for greasing (optional)
- Lemon wedges and tartar sauce for serving

# Air-fried Fish Fingers

🕐 Cooking Time: 10 Min  🍴 Servings: 4

- 400g white fish fillets (such as cod or haddock), cut into finger-sized pieces
- 100g plain flour
- 2 eggs, beaten
- 100g breadcrumbs
- 1 teaspoon paprika
- 1/2 teaspoon garlic powder
- 1/2 teaspoon salt
- 1/2 teaspoon black pepper
- Cooking spray or oil for greasing (optional)
- Lemon wedges and tartar sauce for serving.

## INSTRUCTION

1. Place the plain flour in one bowl, the beaten eggs in another bowl, and the breadcrumbs mixed with garlic powder, paprika, salt, and black pepper in a third bowl.
2. Dredge the scampi tails in the flour, then dip them into the beaten eggs, and finally coat them with the breadcrumb mixture, pressing gently to adhere.
3. If desired, lightly spray or brush the Zone 1 air fryer basket with cooking spray or oil to prevent sticking.
4. Place the breaded scampi tails in Zone 1 of the Ninja Dual Zone Air Fryer, ensuring they are arranged in a single layer.
5. Select Zone 1, choose the AIR FRY program, and set the temperature to 200°C. Set the time to 8-10 minutes.
6. Press the START/STOP button to begin cooking.
7. After 4-5 minutes, carefully turn the scampi tails over for even cooking.
8. Continue cooking for the remaining time or until the scampi tails are golden brown and crispy.
9. Once done, carefully remove the scampi from the air fryer.
10. Serve the **Scampi** hot with lemon wedges and tartar sauce on the side.

1. Place the plain flour in one bowl, the beaten eggs in another bowl, and the breadcrumbs mixed with paprika, garlic powder, salt, and black pepper in a third bowl.
2. Dredge the fish fillet pieces in the flour, then dip them into the beaten eggs, and finally coat them with the breadcrumb mixture, pressing gently to adhere.
3. If desired, lightly spray or brush the Zone 1 air fryer basket with cooking spray or oil to prevent sticking.
4. Place the breaded fish fingers in Zone 1 of the Ninja Dual Zone Air Fryer, ensuring they are arranged in a single layer.
5. Select Zone 1, choose the AIR FRY program, and set the temperature to 200°C. Set the time to 8-10 minutes.
6. Press the START/STOP button to begin cooking.
7. After 4-5 minutes, carefully turn the fish fingers over for even cooking.
8. Continue cooking for the remaining time or until the fish fingers are golden brown and crispy.
9. Once done, carefully remove the fish fingers from the air fryer.
10. Serve the **Fish Fingers** hot with lemon wedges and tartar sauce on the side.

# Air-Fried Sardines

⏱ **Cooking Time: 10 Min**   🍽 **Servings: 4**

- 8 fresh sardines, cleaned and gutted
- 2 tablespoons olive oil
- 1 teaspoon paprika
- 1/2 teaspoon garlic powder
- 1/2 teaspoon salt
- 1/4 teaspoon black pepper
- Lemon wedges for serving

# Cajun Spiced Catfish

⏱ **Cooking Time: 10 Min**   🍽 **Servings: 4**

- 4 catfish fillets
- 2 tablespoons olive oil
- 2 teaspoons Cajun seasoning
- 1/2 teaspoon garlic powder
- 1/2 teaspoon onion powder
- 1/2 teaspoon paprika
- 1/2 teaspoon dried thyme
- 1/2 teaspoon dried oregano
- 1/2 teaspoon salt
- 1/4 teaspoon black pepper
- Lemon wedges for serving

## INSTRUCTION

1. In a small bowl, mix together the olive oil, paprika, garlic powder, salt, and black pepper to create a marinade.
2. Place the cleaned and gutted sardines in a shallow dish and drizzle the marinade over them, making sure they are well coated. Let them marinate for about 10 minutes.
3. If desired, lightly spray or brush the both Zone air fryer basket with cooking spray or oil to prevent sticking.
4. Evenly dividing marinated sardines between the both zone of the Ninja Dual Zone Air Fryer, ensuring they are arranged in a single layer.
5. Select Zone 1, choose the AIR FRY program, and set the temperature to 200°C. Set the time to 8-10 minutes. Select MATCH to duplicate settings across both zones. Press the START/STOP button to begin cooking.
6. After 4-5 minutes, carefully turn the sardines over for even cooking.
7. Continue cooking for the remaining time or until the sardines are cooked through and crispy on the outside.
8. Once done, carefully remove the sardines from the air fryer.
9. Serve the **Air-Fried Sardines** hot with lemon wedges on the side.

1. In a small bowl, mix together the olive oil, Cajun seasoning, garlic powder, onion powder, paprika, dried thyme, dried oregano, salt, and black pepper to create a spice rub.
2. Pat the catfish fillets dry with paper towels and rub the spice mixture evenly over both sides of each fillet.
3. If desired, lightly spray or brush the Zone 1 air fryer basket with cooking spray or oil to prevent sticking.
4. Place the seasoned catfish fillets in Zone 1 of the Ninja Dual Zone Air Fryer, ensuring they are arranged in a single layer.
5. Select Zone 1, choose the AIR FRY program, and set the temperature to 200°C. Set the time to 8-10 minutes.
6. Press the START/STOP button to begin cooking.
7. After 4-5 minutes, carefully turn the catfish fillets over for even cooking.
8. Continue cooking for the remaining time or until the catfish is cooked through and flakes easily with a fork.
9. Once done, carefully remove the catfish fillets from the air fryer.
10. Serve the **Cajun Spiced Catfish** hot with lemon wedges on the side.

# Crispy Haddock Bites

🕐 **Cooking Time: 10 Min**  🍴 **Servings: 4**

- 400g haddock fillets, cut into bite-sized pieces
- 100g breadcrumbs
- 1 teaspoon garlic powder
- 1 teaspoon paprika
- 1/2 teaspoon salt
- 1/2 teaspoon black pepper
- 2 eggs, beaten
- Cooking spray or oil for greasing (optional)
- Lemon wedges for serving

# Lemon Garlic Butter Salmon

🕐 **Cooking Time: 10 Min**  🍴 **Servings: 4**

- 4 salmon fillets
- 2 tablespoons melted butter
- 2 cloves garlic, minced
- 1 tablespoon lemon juice
- 1 teaspoon lemon zest
- 1/2 teaspoon salt
- 1/4 teaspoon black pepper
- Lemon slices for garnish
- Fresh parsley for garnish

## INSTRUCTION

1. In a shallow dish, combine the breadcrumbs, garlic powder, paprika, salt, and black pepper.
2. Dip each haddock bite into the beaten eggs, then coat them evenly with the breadcrumb mixture, pressing gently to adhere.
3. If desired, lightly spray or brush the Zone 1 air fryer basket with cooking spray or oil to prevent sticking.
4. Place the coated haddock bites in Zone 1 of the Ninja Dual Zone Air Fryer, ensuring they are arranged in a single layer.
5. Select Zone 1, choose the AIR FRY program, and set the temperature to 200°C. Set the time to 8-10 minutes.
6. Press the START/STOP button to begin cooking.
7. After 4-5 minutes, carefully turn the haddock bites over for even cooking.
8. Continue cooking for the remaining time or until the haddock bites are golden brown and crispy.
9. Once done, carefully remove the haddock bites from the air fryer.
10. Serve the **Crispy Haddock Bites** hot with lemon wedges on the side.

1. In a small bowl, mix together the melted butter, minced garlic, lemon juice, lemon zest, salt, and black pepper.
2. Place the salmon fillets in Zone 1 of the Ninja Dual Zone Air Fryer, ensuring they are arranged in a single layer.
3. Drizzle the lemon garlic butter mixture evenly over the salmon fillets.
4. Select Zone 1, choose the AIR FRY program, and set the temperature to 200°C. Set the time to 8-10 minutes.
5. Press the START/STOP button to begin cooking.
6. After 4-5 minutes, carefully check the salmon for doneness. The salmon is done when it flakes easily with a fork and reaches an internal temperature of 63°C.
7. Once done, carefully remove the salmon fillets from the air fryer.
8. Garnish the Lemon Garlic Butter Salmon with lemon slices and fresh parsley.
9. Serve the **Lemon Garlic Butter Salmon** hot.

# Teriyaki Glazed Salmon

🕐 **Cooking Time: 10 Min**   🍴 **Servings: 4**

- 4 salmon fillets
- 60ml soy sauce
- 60ml mirin
- 2 tablespoons brown sugar
- 1 tablespoon honey
- 2 cloves garlic, minced
- 1 teaspoon grated ginger
- 1 tablespoon cornstarch
- 1 tablespoon water
- Sesame seeds and chopped green onions for garnish (optional)

# Grilled Swordfish Skewers

🕐 **Cooking Time: 10 Min**   🍴 **Servings: 4**

- 500g swordfish steaks, cut into 2.5 cubes
- 1 tablespoon olive oil
- 2 cloves garlic, minced
- 1 teaspoon paprika
- 1/2 teaspoon ground cumin
- 1/2 teaspoon ground coriander
- 1/2 teaspoon salt
- 1/4 teaspoon black pepper
- 1 lemon, cut into wedges for serving
- Metal or soaked wooden skewers

## INSTRUCTION

1. In a small saucepan, combine the soy sauce, mirin, brown sugar, honey, minced garlic, and grated ginger. Bring to a simmer over medium heat and cook for 2-3 minutes until the sugar has dissolved and the sauce has slightly thickened.
2. In a small bowl, mix the cornstarch and water to make a slurry. Add the slurry to the saucepan and stir well to combine. Cook for another 1-2 minutes until the sauce has thickened further. Remove from heat.
3. Place the salmon fillets in Zone 1 of the Ninja Dual Zone Air Fryer, ensuring they are arranged in a single layer.
4. Brush the teriyaki glaze over the salmon fillets, reserving some for later use.
5. Select Zone 1, choose the AIR FRY program, and set the temperature to 200°C. Set the time to 8-10 minutes. Press the START/STOP.
6. After 4-5 minutes, carefully brush the reserved teriyaki glaze over the salmon fillets.
7. Continue cooking for the remaining time or until the salmon is cooked through and flakes easily with a fork.
8. Once done, carefully remove the salmon fillets from the air fryer.
9. Garnish the **Teriyaki Glazed Salmon** with sesame seeds and chopped green onions, if desired.
10. Serve the Teriyaki Glazed Salmon hot.

1. In a bowl, combine the olive oil, minced garlic, paprika, ground cumin, ground coriander, salt, and black pepper.
2. Add the swordfish cubes to the bowl and toss to coat evenly with the spice mixture.
3. Thread the swordfish cubes onto metal or soaked wooden skewers.
4. If desired, lightly spray or brush the Zone 1 air fryer basket with cooking spray or oil to prevent sticking.
5. Place the swordfish skewers in Zone 1 of the Ninja Dual Zone Air Fryer, ensuring they are arranged in a single layer.
6. Select Zone 1, choose the AIR FRY program, and set the temperature to 200°C. Set the time to 8-10 minutes.
7. Press the START/STOP button to begin cooking.
8. After 4-5 minutes, carefully turn the skewers over for even cooking.
9. Continue cooking for the remaining time or until the swordfish is cooked through and lightly browned on the edges.
10. Once done, carefully remove the swordfish skewers from the air fryer.
11. Serve the **Grilled Swordfish Skewers** hot with lemon wedges on the side.

# Coconut Crusted Cod

🕐 Cooking Time: 10 Min  🍴 Servings: 4

- 4 cod fillets
- 100g shredded coconut
- 50g breadcrumbs
- 2 eggs, beaten
- 1/2 teaspoon garlic powder
- 1/2 teaspoon paprika
- 1/2 teaspoon salt
- 1/4 teaspoon black pepper
- Cooking spray or oil for greasing (optional)
- Lemon wedges for serving

# Pesto-Crusted Halibut

🕐 Cooking Time: 10 Min  🍴 Servings: 4

- 4 halibut fillets
- 4 tablespoons pesto sauce
- 50g breadcrumbs
- 1 tablespoon olive oil
- 1/2 teaspoon garlic powder
- 1/2 teaspoon salt
- 1/4 teaspoon black pepper
- Cooking spray or oil for greasing (optional)
- Lemon wedges for serving

## INSTRUCTION

1. In a shallow dish, mix together the shredded coconut, breadcrumbs, garlic powder, paprika, salt, and black pepper.
2. Dip each cod fillet into the beaten eggs, then coat them evenly with the coconut mixture, pressing gently to adhere.
3. If desired, lightly spray or brush the air fryer basket with cooking spray or oil to prevent sticking.
4. Place the coated cod fillets in Zone 1 of the Ninja Dual Zone Air Fryer, ensuring they are arranged in a single layer.
5. Select Zone 1, choose the AIR FRY program, and set the temperature to 200°C. Set the time to 8-10 minutes.
6. Press the START/STOP button to begin cooking.
7. After 4-5 minutes, carefully turn the cod fillets over for even cooking.
8. Continue cooking for the remaining time or until the coconut crust is golden brown and the cod is cooked through.
9. Once done, carefully remove the cod fillets from the air fryer.
10. Serve the **Coconut Crusted Cod** hot with lemon wedges on the side.

1. In a small bowl, mix together the breadcrumbs, olive oil, garlic powder, salt, and black pepper to create the crust mixture.
2. Spread 1 tablespoon of pesto sauce over each halibut fillet, covering the top evenly.
3. Press the breadcrumb mixture onto the top of each pesto-coated halibut fillet, ensuring it sticks well.
4. If desired, lightly spray or brush the Zone 1 air fryer basket with cooking spray or oil to prevent sticking.
5. Place the halibut fillets in Zone 1 of the Ninja Dual Zone Air Fryer, ensuring they are arranged in a single layer.
6. Select Zone 1, choose the AIR FRY program, and set the temperature to 200°C. Set the time to 8-10 minutes.
7. Press the START/STOP button to begin cooking.
8. After 4-5 minutes, carefully check the halibut fillets for doneness. They should be opaque and flake easily with a fork.
9. Once done, carefully remove the halibut fillets from the air fryer.
10. Serve the **Pesto-Crusted Halibut** hot with lemon wedges on the side.

# Spicy Grilled Mackerel

⏱ **Cooking Time:** 10 Min   🍴 **Servings:** 4

- 4 mackerel fillets
- 2 tablespoons olive oil
- 1 tablespoon soy sauce
- 1 tablespoon lemon juice
- 1 teaspoon paprika
- 1/2 teaspoon cayenne pepper (adjust to taste)
- 1/2 teaspoon garlic powder
- 1/2 teaspoon ground cumin
- 1/2 teaspoon ground coriander
- 1/2 teaspoon salt
- 1/4 teaspoon black pepper
- Lemon wedges for serving

# Herb-crusted Sea Bass

⏱ **Cooking Time:** 10 Min   🍴 **Servings:** 4

- 4 sea bass fillets
- 2 tablespoons olive oil
- 1 tablespoon Dijon mustard
- 60 g breadcrumbs
- 2 tablespoons grated Parmesan cheese
- 1 tablespoon chopped fresh parsley
- 1 tablespoon chopped fresh basil
- 1 tablespoon chopped fresh thyme
- 1/2 teaspoon garlic powder
- 1/2 teaspoon salt
- 1/4 teaspoon black pepper
- Lemon wedges for serving

## INSTRUCTION

1. In a small bowl, whisk together the olive oil, soy sauce, lemon juice, paprika, cayenne pepper, garlic powder, ground cumin, ground coriander, salt, and black pepper to create the marinade.
2. Place the mackerel fillets in a shallow dish and pour the marinade over them, turning to coat evenly. Let them marinate for about 15-20 minutes.
3. Place the marinated mackerel fillets in Zone 1 of the Ninja Dual Zone Air Fryer, ensuring they are arranged in a single layer.
4. Select Zone 1, choose the AIR FRY program, and set the temperature to 200°C. Set the time to 8-10 minutes.
5. Press the START/STOP button to begin cooking.
6. After 4-5 minutes, carefully turn the mackerel fillets over for even cooking.
7. Continue cooking for the remaining time or until the mackerel is cooked through and flakes easily with a fork.
8. Once done, carefully remove the mackerel fillets from the air fryer.
9. Serve the **Spicy Grilled Mackerel** hot with lemon wedges on the side.

1. In a small bowl, mix together the olive oil and Dijon mustard.
2. In another bowl, combine the breadcrumbs, grated Parmesan cheese, chopped fresh parsley, chopped fresh basil, chopped fresh thyme, garlic powder, salt, and black pepper to create the herb crust mixture.
3. Brush each sea bass fillet with the olive oil and Dijon mustard mixture, coating both sides.
4. Press each fillet into the herb crust mixture, coating it evenly on all sides.
5. Place the coated sea bass fillets in Zone 1 of the Ninja Dual Zone Air Fryer, ensuring they are arranged in a single layer.
6. Select Zone 1, choose the AIR FRY program, and set the temperature to 200°C. Set the time to 8-10 minutes.
7. Press the START/STOP button to begin cooking.
8. After 4-5 minutes, carefully turn the sea bass fillets over for even cooking.
9. Continue cooking for the remaining time or until the sea bass is cooked through and the crust is golden brown and crispy.
10. Once done, carefully remove the sea bass fillets from the air fryer.
11. Serve the **Herb-Crusted Sea Bass** hot with lemon wedges on the side.

# Coconut Shrimp

🕐 **Cooking Time:** 10 Min  🍴 **Servings:** 4

- 500g large shrimp, peeled and deveined
- 80 g shredded coconut
- 60 g breadcrumbs
- 2 eggs, beaten
- 1/2 teaspoon garlic powder
- 1/2 teaspoon paprika
- 1/2 teaspoon salt
- 1/4 teaspoon black pepper
- Cooking spray or oil for greasing (optional)
- Sweet chili sauce or mango salsa for dipping

# Smoked Paprika Shrimp

🕐 **Cooking Time:** 10 Min  🍴 **Servings:** 4

- 500g large shrimp, peeled and deveined
- 2 tablespoons olive oil
- 1 teaspoon smoked paprika
- 1/2 teaspoon garlic powder
- 1/2 teaspoon salt
- 1/4 teaspoon black pepper
- Cooking spray or oil for greasing (optional)
- Lemon wedges for serving

## INSTRUCTION

1. In a shallow dish, mix together the shredded coconut, breadcrumbs, garlic powder, paprika, salt, and black pepper.
2. Dip each shrimp into the beaten eggs, then coat them evenly with the coconut mixture, pressing gently to adhere.
3. If desired, lightly spray or brush the Zone 1 air fryer basket with cooking spray or oil to prevent sticking.
4. Place the coated shrimp in Zone 1 of the Ninja Dual Zone Air Fryer, ensuring they are arranged in a single layer.
5. Select Zone 1, choose the AIR FRY program, and set the temperature to 200°C. Set the time to 8-10 minutes.
6. Press the START/STOP button to begin cooking.
7. After 4-5 minutes, carefully turn the shrimp over for even cooking.
8. Continue cooking for the remaining time or until the shrimp is cooked through and the coconut coating is golden brown and crispy.
9. Once done, carefully remove the shrimp from the air fryer.
10. Serve the **Coconut Shrimp** hot with sweet chili sauce or mango salsa for dipping.

1. In a large bowl, toss the shrimp with olive oil, smoked paprika, garlic powder, salt, and black pepper until the shrimp are evenly coated.
2. If desired, lightly spray or brush the Zone 1 air fryer basket with cooking spray or oil to prevent sticking.
3. Place the seasoned shrimp in Zone 1 of the Ninja Dual Zone Air Fryer, ensuring they are arranged in a single layer.
4. Select Zone 1, choose the AIR FRY program, and set the temperature to 200°C. Set the time to 8-10 minutes.
5. Press the START/STOP button to begin cooking.
6. After 4-5 minutes, carefully turn the shrimp over for even cooking.
7. Continue cooking for the remaining time or until the shrimp are pink and opaque.
8. Once done, carefully remove the shrimp from the air fryer.
9. Serve the **Smoked Paprika Shrimp** hot with lemon wedges on the side.

# Garlic Butter Shrimp

🕐 **Cooking Time:** 10 Min   🍴 **Servings:** 4

- 500g large shrimp, peeled and deveined
- 4 tablespoons unsalted butter
- 4 cloves garlic, minced
- 1 tablespoon lemon juice
- 1/2 teaspoon paprika
- 1/2 teaspoon salt
- 1/4 teaspoon black pepper
- Cooking spray or oil for greasing (optional)
- Chopped fresh parsley for garnish
- Lemon wedges for serving

# Crispy Prawn Balls

🕐 **Cooking Time:** 10 Min   🍴 **Servings:** 4

- 500g prawns, peeled and deveined
- 1 egg, beaten
- 60g breadcrumbs
- 2 tablespoons cornflour
- 1 teaspoon garlic powder
- 1/2 teaspoon salt
- 1/4 teaspoon black pepper
- Cooking spray or oil for greasing (optional)
- Sweet chili sauce or tartar sauce for dipping

## INSTRUCTION

1. In a small saucepan, melt the butter over medium heat. Add the minced garlic and cook for 1-2 minutes until fragrant.
2. Stir in the lemon juice, paprika, salt, and black pepper. Remove from heat and let the garlic butter mixture cool slightly.
3. In a large bowl, toss the shrimp with the garlic butter mixture until evenly coated.
4. If desired, lightly spray or brush the Zone 1 air fryer basket with cooking spray or oil to prevent sticking.
5. Place the garlic butter-coated shrimp in Zone 1 of the Ninja Dual Zone Air Fryer, ensuring they are arranged in a single layer.
6. Select Zone 1, choose the AIR FRY program, and set the temperature to 200°C. Set the time to 8-10 minutes.
7. Press the START/STOP button to begin cooking.
8. After 4-5 minutes, carefully turn the shrimp over for even cooking.
9. Continue cooking for the remaining time or until the shrimp are pink and opaque.
10. Once done, carefully remove the shrimp from the air fryer.
11. Serve the **Garlic Butter Shrimp** hot, garnished with chopped fresh parsley and lemon wedges on the side.

1. In a food processor, pulse the prawns until finely chopped but not pureed.
2. Transfer the chopped prawns to a bowl and add the beaten egg, breadcrumbs, cornflour, garlic powder, salt, and black pepper. Mix until well combined.
3. Shape the prawn mixture into small balls, about 2,5cm in diameter.
4. If desired, lightly spray or brush the Zone 1 air fryer basket with cooking spray or oil to prevent sticking.
5. Place the prawn balls in Zone 1 of the Ninja Dual Zone Air Fryer, ensuring they are arranged in a single layer.
6. Select Zone 1, choose the AIR FRY program, and set the temperature to 200°C. Set the time to 8-10 minutes.
7. Press the START/STOP button to begin cooking.
8. After 4-5 minutes, carefully turn the prawn balls over for even cooking.
9. Continue cooking for the remaining time or until the prawn balls are golden brown and crispy.
10. Once done, carefully remove the prawn balls from the air fryer.
11. Serve the **Crispy Prawn Balls** hot with sweet chili sauce or tartar sauce for dipping.

## Piri-piri Prawns

⏱ Cooking Time: 10 Min  🍴 Servings: 4

- 500g large prawns, peeled and deveined
- 2 tablespoons olive oil
- 2 tablespoons lemon juice
- 2 cloves garlic, minced
- 1 teaspoon paprika
- 1/2 teaspoon dried oregano
- 1/2 teaspoon dried thyme
- 1/2 teaspoon salt
- 1/4 teaspoon black pepper
- Cooking spray or oil for greasing (optional)
- Lemon wedges for serving

## Cajun Shrimp Skewers

⏱ Cooking Time: 10 Min  🍴 Servings: 4

- 500g large shrimp, peeled and deveined
- 2 tablespoons olive oil
- 1 tablespoon Cajun seasoning
- 1/2 teaspoon garlic powder
- 1/2 teaspoon onion powder
- 1/2 teaspoon paprika
- 1/4 teaspoon cayenne pepper (adjust to taste)
- 1/2 teaspoon salt
- 1/4 teaspoon black pepper
- Cooking spray or oil for greasing (optional)
- Lemon wedges for serving

## INSTRUCTION

1. In a bowl, mix together the olive oil, lemon juice, minced garlic, paprika, dried oregano, dried thyme, salt, and black pepper to make the marinade.
2. Add the prawns to the marinade and toss to coat evenly.
3. If desired, lightly spray or brush the Zone 1 air fryer basket with cooking spray or oil to prevent sticking.
4. Place the marinated prawns in Zone 1 of the Ninja Dual Zone Air Fryer, ensuring they are arranged in a single layer.
5. Select Zone 1, choose the AIR FRY program, and set the temperature to 200°C. Set the time to 8-10 minutes.
6. Press the START/STOP button to begin cooking.
7. After 4-5 minutes, carefully turn the prawns over for even cooking.
8. Continue cooking for the remaining time or until the prawns are pink and opaque.
9. Once done, carefully remove the prawns from the air fryer.
10. Serve the **Piri-Piri Prawns** hot with lemon wedges on the side.

1. In a bowl, combine the olive oil, Cajun seasoning, garlic powder, onion powder, paprika, cayenne pepper, salt, and black pepper.
2. Add the shrimp to the bowl and toss to coat evenly with the seasoning mixture.
3. If using wooden skewers, soak them in water for about 30 minutes to prevent burning.
4. Thread the seasoned shrimp onto the skewers, dividing them evenly.
5. If desired, lightly spray or brush the Zone 1 air fryer basket with cooking spray or oil to prevent sticking.
6. Place the shrimp skewers in Zone 1 of the Ninja Dual Zone Air Fryer, ensuring they are arranged in a single layer.
7. Select Zone 1, choose the AIR FRY program, and set the temperature to 200°C. Set the time to 8-10 minutes.
8. Press the START/STOP button to begin cooking.
9. After 4-5 minutes, carefully turn the skewers over for even cooking.
10. Continue cooking for the remaining time or until the shrimp are pink and opaque.
11. Once done, carefully remove the shrimp skewers from the air fryer.
12. Serve the **Cajun Shrimp Skewers** hot with lemon wedges on the side.

# Spicy Cajun Crawfish

⏱ **Cooking Time:** 10 Min  🍴 **Servings:** 4

- 500g crawfish tails, peeled and deveined
- 2 tablespoons olive oil
- 1 tablespoon Cajun seasoning
- 1/2 teaspoon garlic powder
- 1/2 teaspoon onion powder
- 1/2 teaspoon paprika
- 1/4 teaspoon cayenne pepper (adjust to taste)
- 1/2 teaspoon salt
- 1/4 teaspoon black pepper
- Cooking spray or oil for greasing (optional)
- Lemon wedges for serving

# Tandoori Fish Tikka

⏱ **Cooking Time:** 10 Min  🍴 **Servings:** 4

- 500g firm white fish fillets, cut into chunks
- 1 cup plain yogurt (about 240g)
- 2 tablespoons lemon juice
- 2 teaspoons tandoori masala spice mix
- 1 teaspoon ground cumin
- 1 teaspoon ground coriander
- 1/2 teaspoon paprika
- 1/2 teaspoon turmeric
- 1/2 teaspoon salt
- 1/4 teaspoon black pepper
- 2 cloves garlic, minced
- 2.5 cm piece of ginger, grated
- Lemon wedges and chopped fresh coriander for serving

## INSTRUCTION

1. In a bowl, combine the olive oil, Cajun seasoning, garlic powder, onion powder, paprika, cayenne pepper, salt, and black pepper.
2. Add the crawfish tails to the bowl and toss to coat evenly with the seasoning mixture.
3. If desired, lightly spray or brush the Zone 1 air fryer basket with cooking spray or oil to prevent sticking.
4. Place the seasoned crawfish tails in Zone 1 of the Ninja Dual Zone Air Fryer, ensuring they are arranged in a single layer.
5. Select Zone 1, choose the AIR FRY program, and set the temperature to 200°C. Set the time to 8-10 minutes.
6. Press the START/STOP button to begin cooking.
7. After 4-5 minutes, carefully turn the crawfish tails over for even cooking.
8. Continue cooking for the remaining time or until the crawfish tails are heated through.
9. Once done, carefully remove the crawfish tails from the air fryer.
10. Serve the **Spicy Cajun Crawfish** hot with lemon wedges on the side.

1. In a bowl, combine the yogurt, lemon juice, tandoori masala spice mix, ground cumin, ground coriander, paprika, turmeric, salt, black pepper, minced garlic, and grated ginger. Mix well to form a marinade.
2. Add the fish chunks to the marinade, making sure they are well coated. Cover and refrigerate for at least 1 hour to marinate.
3. Thread the marinated fish chunks onto skewers, dividing them evenly.
4. Place the fish skewers in Zone 1 of the Ninja Dual Zone Air Fryer, ensuring they are arranged in a single layer.
5. Select Zone 1, choose the AIR FRY program, and set the temperature to 180°C. Set the time to 8-10 minutes.
6. Press the START/STOP button to begin cooking.
7. After 4-5 minutes, carefully turn the fish skewers over for even cooking.
8. Continue cooking for the remaining time or until the fish is cooked through and slightly charred around the edges.
9. Once done, carefully remove the fish skewers from the air fryer.
10. Serve the **Tandoori Fish Tikka** hot with lemon wedges and chopped fresh coriander.

## Beer battered Haddock

🕐 **Cooking Time: 10 Min** 🍴 **Servings: 4**

- 4 haddock fillets, skin removed
- 1 cup all-purpose flour (about 120g)
- 1 teaspoon baking powder
- 1/2 teaspoon salt
- 1/4 teaspoon black pepper
- 1 cup beer (about 240ml)
- Cooking spray or oil for greasing (optional)
- Lemon wedges and tartar sauce for serving

## Salt & Pepper Squid

🕐 **Cooking Time: 10 Min** 🍴 **Servings: 4**

- 500g fresh squid tubes, cleaned and sliced into rings
- 1/2 cup cornflour (about 60g)
- 1 teaspoon sea salt
- 1 teaspoon ground black pepper
- 1/2 teaspoon Chinese five-spice powder
- 2 tablespoons vegetable oil
- Cooking spray or oil for greasing (optional)
- Lemon wedges and sweet chili sauce for serving

## INSTRUCTION

1. In a bowl, whisk together the all-purpose flour, baking powder, salt, and black pepper.
2. Gradually whisk in the beer until the batter is smooth and has the consistency of pancake batter.
3. Dip each haddock fillet into the batter, coating it completely.
4. If desired, lightly spray or brush the Zone 1 air fryer basket with cooking spray or oil to prevent sticking.
5. Place the battered haddock fillets in Zone 1 of the Ninja Dual Zone Air Fryer, ensuring they are arranged in a single layer.
6. Select Zone 1, choose the AIR FRY program, and set the temperature to 200°C. Set the time to 8-10 minutes.
7. Press the START/STOP button to begin cooking.
8. After 4-5 minutes, carefully turn the haddock fillets over for even cooking.
9. Continue cooking for the remaining time or until the batter is golden brown and the fish is cooked through.
10. Once done, carefully remove the beer battered haddock fillets from the air fryer.
11. Serve the **Beer Battered Haddock** hot with lemon wedges and tartar sauce on the side.

1. In a bowl, combine the cornflour, sea salt, black pepper, and Chinese five-spice powder.
2. Toss the squid rings in the cornflour mixture until they are well coated.
3. If desired, lightly spray or brush the Zone 1 air fryer basket with cooking spray or oil to prevent sticking.
4. Place the coated squid rings in Zone 1 of the Ninja Dual Zone Air Fryer, ensuring they are arranged in a single layer.
5. Select Zone 1, choose the AIR FRY program, and set the temperature to 200°C. Set the time to 8-10 minutes.
6. Press the START/STOP button to begin cooking.
7. After 4-5 minutes, carefully turn the squid rings over for even cooking.
8. Continue cooking for the remaining time or until the squid rings are golden brown and crispy.
9. Once done, carefully remove the salt and pepper squid from the air fryer.
10. Serve the **Salt and Pepper Squid** hot with lemon wedges and sweet chili sauce on the side.

# Apple Crisp

⏱ **Cooking Time:** 30 Min   🍽 **Servings:** 4

- 4 medium-sized apples, peeled, cored, and sliced
- 50g granulated sugar
- 1 tsp ground cinnamon
- 1/2 tsp ground nutmeg
- 100g plain flour
- 50g rolled oats
- 100g unsalted butter, cold and diced
- 50g light brown sugar

# Banana Fritters

⏱ **Cooking Time:** 10 Min   🍽 **Servings:** 12 banana fritters

- 2 ripe bananas, mashed
- 100g all-purpose flour
- 1 tsp baking powder
- 2 tbsp granulated sugar
- 1/2 tsp ground cinnamon
- A pinch of salt
- 1 large egg
- 60ml milk
- 1/2 tsp vanilla extract
- Vegetable oil or non-stick cooking spray for greasing
- Icing sugar for dusting (optional)

## INSTRUCTION

1. In a large bowl, combine the sliced apples, granulated sugar, cinnamon, and nutmeg. Toss until the apples are evenly coated.
2. In a separate bowl, mix the flour, oats, and brown sugar. Add the cold diced butter and rub it into the flour mixture using your fingertips until it resembles coarse breadcrumbs.
3. Place the coated apple slices in a baking dish that fits into Zone 1 of the air fryer.
4. Sprinkle the crumb mixture evenly over the apples.
5. Place the baking dish in Zone 1 of the Ninja Dual Zone Air Fryer.
6. Select Zone 1, choose the BAKE program, and set the temperature to 180°C. Set the time to 25-30 minutes.
7. Press the START/STOP button to begin cooking.
8. Check the crisp after 25 minutes. If the topping is golden brown and the apples are tender, it's ready. If not, continue cooking for an additional 5 minutes.
9. Once done, carefully remove the baking dish from the air fryer and let it cool for a few minutes before serving.
10. Serve the **Apple Crisp** warm, optionally with a scoop of vanilla ice cream

1. In a mixing bowl, combine the mashed bananas, flour, baking powder, sugar, cinnamon, and salt.
2. In a separate bowl, whisk together the egg, milk, and vanilla extract.
3. Pour the wet ingredients into the dry ingredients and stir until just combined. Be careful not to overmix.
4. Lightly grease the air fryer basket or trays with vegetable oil or non-stick cooking spray.
5. Using a spoon or cookie scoop, drop spoonfuls of the batter into the air fryer basket or trays, leaving some space between each fritter.
6. Select Zone 1, choose the AIR FRY program, and set the temperature to 180°C. Set the time to 8-10 minutes.
7. Press the START/STOP button to begin cooking.
8. After 4-5 minutes, carefully flip the fritters using tongs or a spatula to ensure even cooking.
9. Continue cooking for another 4-5 minutes until the fritters are golden brown and crispy.
10. Once done, carefully remove the **banana fritters** from the air fryer and let them cool for a few minutes.
11. Dust with icing sugar if desired before serving.

# Bread Pudding

🕐 **Cooking Time: 30 Min**   🍴 **Servings: 6**

- 300g stale bread, torn into small pieces
- 500ml whole milk
- 2 large eggs
- 100g granulated sugar
- 1 tsp vanilla extract
- 1/2 tsp ground cinnamon
- 1/4 tsp ground nutmeg
- 50g raisins (optional)
- Butter or non-stick cooking spray for greasing

# Brownies

🕐 **Cooking Time: 25 Min**   🍴 **Servings: 9-12 brownies**

- 100g unsalted butter, melted
- 200g granulated sugar
- 2 large eggs
- 1 tsp vanilla extract
- 60g plain flour
- 40g unsweetened cocoa powder
- 1/4 tsp baking powder
- A pinch of salt
- 50g chopped walnuts or pecans (optional)

## INSTRUCTION

1. In a large bowl, soak the torn bread in the milk for about 15-20 minutes, or until the bread has absorbed most of the milk.
2. In another bowl, whisk together the eggs, sugar, vanilla extract, cinnamon, and nutmeg.
3. Add the egg mixture to the soaked bread and mix until well combined. If using raisins, fold them into the mixture.
4. Grease a baking dish that fits into Zone 1 of the air fryer with butter or non-stick cooking spray.
5. Transfer the bread pudding mixture into the greased baking dish.
6. Place the baking dish in Zone 1 of the air fryer.
7. Select Zone 1, choose the BAKE program, and set the temperature to 160°C. Set the time to 25-30 minutes.
8. Press the START/STOP button to begin cooking.
9. Check the bread pudding after 25 minutes. It should be set and golden brown on top. If not, continue cooking for an additional 5 minutes.
10. Once done, carefully remove the baking dish from the air fryer and let the bread pudding cool for a few minutes before serving.
11. Serve the **Bread Pudding** warm, optionally with a drizzle of custard or a sprinkle of powdered sugar.

1. In a mixing bowl, whisk together the melted butter and sugar until well combined.
2. Add the eggs and vanilla extract to the butter-sugar mixture. Whisk until smooth.
3. In a separate bowl, sift together the flour, cocoa powder, baking powder, and salt.
4. Gradually add the dry ingredients to the wet ingredients, mixing until just combined. Be careful not to overmix.
5. If using nuts, fold them into the batter.
6. Grease a baking dish that fits into Zone 1 of the air fryer with butter or non-stick cooking spray.
7. Transfer the brownie batter into the greased baking dish.
8. Place the baking dish in Zone 1 of the air fryer.
9. Select Zone 1, choose the BAKE program, and set the temperature to 160°C. Set the time to 20-25 minutes.
10. Press the START/STOP button to begin cooking.
11. Check the brownies after 20 minutes. They should be set around the edges and slightly gooey in the center. If they're not done, continue cooking for an additional 3-5 minutes.
12. Once done, carefully remove the baking dish from the air fryer and let the **brownies** cool completely before cutting into squares.

# Chocolate Chip Cookies

**Cooking Time:** 8 Min  **Servings:** 4

- 115g unsalted butter, softened
- 100g granulated sugar
- 100g light brown sugar
- 1 large egg
- 1 tsp vanilla extract
- 200g plain flour
- 1/2 tsp baking soda
- A pinch of salt
- 150g chocolate chips

# Churros

**Cooking Time:** 10 Min  **Servings:** 12-16 churros

- 250ml water
- 115g unsalted butter
- 1 tbsp granulated sugar
- 1/4 tsp salt
- 180g plain flour
- 2 large eggs
- 1/2 tsp vanilla extract
- Granulated sugar for coating
- Ground cinnamon for coating
- Vegetable oil or non-stick cooking spray

## INSTRUCTION

1. In a mixing bowl, cream together the softened butter, granulated sugar, and light brown sugar until light and fluffy.
2. Add the egg and vanilla extract to the creamed mixture. Beat until well combined.
3. In a separate bowl, sift together the flour, baking soda, and salt.
4. Gradually add the dry ingredients to the wet ingredients, mixing until just combined.
5. Fold in the chocolate chips until evenly distributed throughout the dough.
6. Line the air fryer basket or trays with parchment paper.
7. Using a spoon or cookie scoop, drop spoonfuls of cookie dough onto the lined basket or trays, leaving some space between each cookie for spreading.
8. Place the basket or trays in Zone 1 of the air fryer.
9. Select Zone 1, choose the BAKE program, and set the temperature to 160°C. Set the time to 8-10 minutes. Press the START/STOP.
10. Check the cookies after 8 minutes. They should be golden brown around the edges and slightly soft in the center. If they're not done, continue cooking for an additional 1-2 minutes.
11. Once done, carefully remove the **cookies** from the air fryer and let them cool on a wire rack.

1. In a saucepan, combine the water, butter, sugar, and salt. Bring to a boil over medium heat.
2. Remove the saucepan from the heat and add the flour. Stir vigorously until the mixture forms a ball of dough.
3. Transfer the dough to a mixing bowl and let it cool for a few minutes.
4. Add the eggs, one at a time, to the dough, mixing well after each addition. Stir in the vanilla extract until the dough is smooth and well combined.
5. Grease the air fryer basket or trays with vegetable oil or non-stick cooking spray.
6. Transfer the churro dough to a piping bag fitted with a large star tip.
7. Pipe the dough onto the greased basket or trays in long strips, cutting them with scissors into desired lengths.
8. Place the basket or trays in Zone 1 of the air fryer.
9. Select Zone 1, choose the AIR FRY program, and set the temperature to 180°C. Set the time to 8-10 minutes. Press the START/STOP.
10. Check the churros after 8 minutes. They should be golden brown and crispy. If they're not done, continue cooking for an additional 1-2 minutes.
11. Once done, carefully remove the **churros** from the air fryer and let them cool for a few minutes.
12. In a shallow dish, mix granulated sugar and ground cinnamon for coating. Roll the warm churros in the sugar-cinnamon mixture until coated.

# Cinnamon Rolls

🕐 **Cooking Time:** 12 Min  🍴 **Servings:** 8 cinnamon rolls.

- 300g all-purpose flour
- 50g granulated sugar
- 1 tsp instant yeast
- 1/4 tsp salt
- 120ml warm milk
- 40g melted unsalted butter
- 1 large egg
- 1 tsp vanilla extract

**Filling:**
- 50g softened unsalted butter
- 50g brown sugar
- 1 tbsp ground cinnamon

**Glaze:**
- 100g icing sugar
- 1-2 tbsp milk
- 1/2 tsp vanilla extract

## INSTRUCTION

1. Mix dry ingredients in a bowl. Mix dry ingredients in a bowl.
2. Pour the wet ingredients into the dry ingredients and mix until a dough forms.
3. Turn the dough out onto a lightly floured surface and knead for about 5-7 minutes until smooth and elastic.
4. Place the dough in a greased bowl, cover with a clean kitchen towel, and let it rise in a warm place for about 1 hour or until doubled in size.
5. Punch down the dough to release the air. Roll out the dough into a rectangle, about 30x20cm in size.
6. Spread the softened butter over the dough, then sprinkle the brown sugar and cinnamon evenly over the buttered surface. Starting from the long side, tightly roll up the dough into a log. Cut log into 8 pieces.
7. Place the cinnamon rolls into both Zone, ensuring they are not touching. Select Zone 1, choose the AIR FRY program, set the temperature to 180°C. Set time to 10-12 minutes. Select MATCH. Press the START/STOP.
8. While the cinnamon rolls are cooking, Mix glaze ingredients until smooth.
9. After 5 minutes, carefully rotate the cinnamon rolls for even cooking. Continue cooking for another 5-7 minutes, or until the cinnamon rolls are golden brown and cooked through.
10. Once done, drizzle the glaze over the warm **cinnamon rolls** and Serve.

# Donuts

🕐 **Cooking Time:** 10 Min  🍴 **Servings:** 8-10 donuts and holes

- 250g all-purpose flour
- 50g granulated sugar
- 7g instant yeast
- 1/4 tsp salt
- 120ml warm milk
- 1 large egg
- 30g unsalted butter, melted
- 1 tsp vanilla extract
- Vegetable oil or non-stick cooking spray

**For the Glaze:**
- 200g icing sugar
- 3-4 tbsp milk
- 1 tsp vanilla extract
- Food coloring (optional)

## INSTRUCTION

1. In a bowl, combine flour, sugar, yeast, and salt.
2. Add warm milk, egg, melted butter, and vanilla extract to the dry ingredients. Mix into a soft dough.
3. Knead the dough for 5 minutes, then let it rise for 1 hour until doubled.
4. Roll out the dough on a floured surface to about 1.5 cm thick.
5. Use a donut cutter or two differently sized round cutters to cut out donuts and donut holes.
6. Evenly dividing donuts and holes into trays or baskets of both zone of the air fryer.
7. Select Zone 1, choose the AIR FRY program, and set the temperature to 180°C. Set the time to 6-8 minutes ( until golden brown). Select MATCH to duplicate settings across both zones. Press the START/STOP.
8. Flipping halfway through for even cooking.
9. Remove the donuts from the air fryer and let them cool on a wire rack.
10. For the glaze, whisk together icing sugar, milk, and vanilla extract until smooth. Add food coloring if desired.
11. Dip each cooled **donut** into the glaze, then place them back on the wire rack to set.

# Eclairs

**Cooking Time:** 15 Min  **Servings:** 8 eclairs

- 120ml water
- 60g unsalted butter
- 1/4 tsp salt
- 1 tsp granulated sugar
- 70g all-purpose flour
- 2 large eggs
- 240ml heavy cream
- 1 tsp vanilla extract
- 100g dark chocolate, chopped
- 1 tbsp unsalted butter
- 1-2 tbsp powdered sugar for dusting (optional)

# Fruit Crumble

**Cooking Time:** 25 Min  **Servings:** 4

- 500g mixed fruit (e.g., apples, berries, peaches), peeled and sliced if necessary
- 50g granulated sugar (adjust to taste)
- 1 tbsp lemon juice
- 50g all-purpose flour
- 50g rolled oats
- 50g unsalted butter, chilled and cubed
- 50g brown sugar
- 1/2 tsp ground cinnamon
- A pinch of salt

## INSTRUCTION

1. In a saucepan, combine water, butter, salt, and sugar. Bring to a boil.
2. Reduce heat to low and add flour all at once, stirring vigorously until mixture forms a ball. Remove from heat and let cool for 5 minutes. Add eggs, one at a time, beating well after each addition until smooth.
3. Transfer the dough to a piping bag fitted with a round tip. Pipe the dough into 7 cm strips onto a greased tray, leaving space between each eclair.
4. Place the tray in both Zone of the air fryer basket.
5. Select Zone 1, choose the AIR FRY program, and set the temperature to 200°C. Set the time to 12-15 minutes. Select MATCH. Press the START/STOP.
6. While the eclairs are baking, whip the heavy cream with vanilla extract until stiff peaks form.
7. Once the eclairs are golden brown and puffed, remove them from the air fryer and let them cool on a wire rack.
8. Once cooled, slice the eclairs in half horizontally.
9. Fill each eclair with whipped cream using a piping bag or spoon.
10. In a microwave-safe bowl, melt the chopped chocolate and butter in short intervals, stirring until smooth.
11. Dip the top of each filled **eclair** into the melted chocolate, allowing any excess to drip off.
12. Place the dipped eclairs on a tray and refrigerate for 30 minutes to set the chocolate. Dust with powdered sugar before serving, if desired.

1. In a bowl, combine the mixed fruit, granulated sugar, and lemon juice. Toss until the fruit is evenly coated. Adjust the sugar to taste depending on the sweetness of the fruit.
2. In another bowl, mix the flour, oats, brown sugar, cinnamon, and salt.
3. Add the chilled butter cubes to the flour mixture. Use your fingertips to rub the butter into the dry ingredients until it resembles coarse breadcrumbs.
4. Transfer the fruit mixture to a greased baking dish that fits into Zone 1 of the air fryer.
5. Sprinkle the crumble mixture evenly over the fruit.
6. Place the baking dish in Zone 1 of the air fryer.
7. Select Zone 1, choose the BAKE program, and set the temperature to 180°C. Set the time to 20-25 minutes.
8. Press the START/STOP button to begin cooking.
9. Check the crumble after 20 minutes. The topping should be golden brown and the fruit bubbling.
10. Once done, carefully remove the baking dish from the air fryer and let the crumble cool for a few minutes.
11. Serve the **Fruit Crumble** warm, optionally with a scoop of vanilla ice cream or a dollop of whipped cream.

## Lemon Bars

🕐 **Cooking Time:** 25 Min  🍴 **Servings:** 12 lemon bars.

- 150g all-purpose flour
- 50g powdered sugar
- A pinch of salt
- 115g unsalted butter, cold and cubed
- 2 large eggs
- 200g granulated sugar
- 30g all-purpose flour
- Zest of 1 lemon
- 80ml freshly squeezed lemon juice
- Powdered sugar, for dusting

## Mini Cheesecakes

🕐 **Cooking Time:** 20 Min  🍴 **Servings:** 12 mini cheesecakes.

- 200g digestive biscuits, crushed
- 50g unsalted butter, melted
- 225g cream cheese, softened
- 50g granulated sugar
- 1 large egg
- 1/2 tsp vanilla extract
- 100ml sour cream
- Fruit preserves or fresh berries for topping (optional)

## INSTRUCTION

1. In a bowl, combine 150g flour, powdered sugar, and a pinch of salt.
2. Add the cold cubed butter to the flour mixture. Use your fingertips to rub the butter into the dry ingredients until it resembles coarse crumbs.
3. Press the mixture into the bottom of a greased baking dish that fits into Zone 1 of the air fryer.
4. Bake in Zone 1 using the BAKE program for 15-20 minutes or until lightly golden.
5. While the crust is baking, prepare the lemon filling.
6. In a bowl, whisk together the eggs, granulated sugar, 30g flour, lemon zest, and lemon juice until well combined.
7. Once the crust is baked, pour the lemon filling over the hot crust.
8. Return the baking dish to Zone 1 of the air fryer.
9. Select Zone 1, choose the BAKE program, and set the temperature to 160°C. Set the time to 20-25 minutes.
10. Press the START/STOP button to begin cooking.
11. Check the lemon bars after 20 minutes. The filling should be set but slightly jiggly in the center.
12. Once done, carefully remove the baking dish from the air fryer and let the lemon bars cool completely.
13. Dust the cooled **lemon bars** with powdered sugar before cutting into squares.

1. In a bowl, mix the crushed digestive biscuits with melted butter until well combined.
2. Line the bottom of the baking dish that fits into Zone 1 of the air fryer with cupcake liners.
3. Divide the biscuit mixture evenly among the cupcake liners, pressing down firmly to form the crust.
4. In another bowl, beat the cream cheese and sugar until smooth.
5. Add the egg and vanilla extract, and beat until well combined.
6. Add the sour cream and mix until smooth.
7. Pour the cream cheese mixture over the biscuit crusts in the cupcake liners, filling each about 3/4 full.
8. Evenly dividing baking dish between the two zone.
9. Select Zone 1, choose the BAKE program, and set the temperature to 160°C. Set the time to 15-18 minutes. Select MATCH. Press the START/STOP button to begin cooking.
10. Check the mini cheesecakes after 15 minutes. They should be set but slightly jiggly in the center.
11. Once done, carefully remove the baking dish from the air fryer and let the mini cheesecakes cool in the refrigerator for at least 2 hours or until set.
12. Before serving, top each **mini cheesecake** with a dollop of fruit preserves or fresh berries if desired.

# Peach Cobbler

🕐 **Cooking Time:** 25 Min  🍴 **Servings:** 6

- 4 large peaches, peeled, pitted, and sliced
- 100g granulated sugar
- 1 tbsp lemon juice
- 1/2 tsp vanilla extract
- 50g unsalted butter, melted
- 100g all-purpose flour
- 1 tsp baking powder
- A pinch of salt
- 100ml milk
- Ground cinnamon for dusting
- Vanilla ice cream or whipped cream for serving (optional)

# Pineapple Upside-Down Cake

🕐 **Cooking Time:** 30 Min  🍴 **Servings:** 6-8

- 6-8 pineapple rings, canned or fresh
- 6-8 maraschino cherries
- 100g unsalted butter, melted
- 100g light brown sugar
- 2 large eggs
- 100g granulated sugar
- 1 tsp vanilla extract
- 120ml pineapple juice (reserved from the canned pineapple)
- 150g all-purpose flour
- 1 1/2 tsp baking powder
- A pinch of salt

## INSTRUCTION

1. In a bowl, combine the sliced peaches, granulated sugar, lemon juice, and vanilla extract. Toss until the peaches are coated, then set aside.
2. Pour the melted butter into a greased baking dish that fits into Zone 1 of the air fryer.
3. In a separate bowl, mix the flour, baking powder, and salt.
4. Gradually add the milk to the flour mixture, stirring until smooth.
5. Pour the batter over the melted butter in the baking dish.
6. Arrange the peach slices on top of the batter.
7. Sprinkle ground cinnamon over the peaches.
8. Place the baking dish in Zone 1 of the air fryer.
9. Select Zone 1, choose the BAKE program, and set the temperature to 180°C. Set the time to 20-25 minutes.
10. Press the START/STOP button to begin cooking.
11. Check the peach cobbler after 20 minutes. The topping should be golden brown and the peaches bubbling.
12. Once done, carefully remove the baking dish from the air fryer and let the peach cobbler cool for a few minutes.
13. Serve the **Peach Cobbler** warm, optionally with a scoop of vanilla ice cream or a dollop of whipped cream.

---

1. Grease the bottom of a round baking dish that fits into Zone 1 of the air fryer.
2. Arrange the pineapple rings in the bottom of the baking dish, placing a maraschino cherry in the center of each ring. Set aside.
3. In a bowl, cream together the melted butter and light brown sugar. Spread this mixture evenly over the pineapple rings in the baking dish.
4. In another bowl, beat the eggs, granulated sugar, and vanilla extract until light and fluffy.
5. Gradually add the pineapple juice to the egg mixture, beating until well combined.
6. In a separate bowl, sift together the flour, baking powder, and salt.
7. Gradually add the dry ingredients to the wet ingredients, mixing until just combined.
8. Pour the batter over the pineapple rings and smooth the top with a spatula.
9. Place the baking dish in Zone 1 of the air fryer.
10. Select Zone 1, choose the BAKE program, set the temperature to 160°C, set the time to 25-30 minutes. Press the START/STOP.
11. Check the cake after 25 minutes. It should be golden brown and a toothpick inserted into the center should come out clean.
12. Once done, let the cake cool in the dish for a few minutes. Place a serving plate **upside down** over the baking dish, then carefully invert the cake onto the plate.

# Shortbread Cookies

⏱ Cooking Time: 10 Min    🍴 Servings: 24 cookies

- 225g unsalted butter, softened
- 100g granulated sugar
- 1 tsp vanilla extract
- 250g all-purpose flour
- 50g cornstarch
- A pinch of salt

# S'mores

⏱ Cooking Time: 5 Min    🍴 Servings: 2

- Graham crackers, broken in half
- Milk chocolate squares
- Large marshmallows

## INSTRUCTION

1. In a bowl, cream together the softened butter and granulated sugar until light and fluffy.
2. Add the vanilla extract to the creamed mixture and mix until well combined.
3. In another bowl, sift together the all-purpose flour, cornstarch, and salt.
4. Gradually add the dry ingredients to the creamed mixture, mixing until a dough forms.
5. Roll out the dough on a lightly floured surface to about 0.8 cm thickness.
6. Use cookie cutters to cut out shapes from the dough.
7. Place the cookies on a greased tray or basket that fits into each Zone of the air fryer, evenly dividing them between the two zone, leaving some space between each cookie.
8. Select Zone 1, choose the BAKE program, and set the temperature to 160°C. Set the time to 8-10 minutes.
9. Select MATCH to duplicate settings across both zones. Press the START/STOP.
10. Check the **cookies** after 8 minutes. They should be lightly golden around the edges.
11. Once done, carefully remove the tray or basket from the air fryer and let the cookies cool on a wire rack.

1. Place half of the graham crackers on a baking tray or in the air fryer basket that fits into Zone 1 of the air fryer.
2. Top each graham cracker with a piece of milk chocolate.
3. Place a marshmallow on top of the chocolate.
4. Place the tray or basket in Zone 1 of the air fryer.
5. Select Zone 1, choose the AIR FRY program, and set the temperature to 180°C. Set the time to 3-5 minutes.
6. Press the START/STOP button to begin cooking.
7. Watch the S'mores closely as they cook. Once the marshmallows are toasted to your liking and the chocolate is melted, remove the tray or basket from the air fryer.
8. Carefully place the remaining graham cracker halves on top of the marshmallows to form sandwiches.
9. Serve the **S'mores** immediately while they're warm and gooey.

# Sticky Toffee Pudding

**Cooking Time:** 30 Min   **Servings:** 8

- 200g pitted dates, chopped
- 250ml boiling water
- 1 tsp vanilla extract
- 100g unsalted butter, softened
- 150g light brown sugar
- 2 large eggs
- 200g self-raising flour
- 1/2 tsp baking soda
- A pinch of salt

**For the Toffee Sauce:**
- 100g unsalted butter
- 150g light brown sugar
- 150ml double cream

# Strawberry Shortcake

**Cooking Time:** 12 Min   **Servings:** 8

- 450g fresh strawberries, hulled and sliced
- 50g granulated sugar
- 1 tsp lemon juice
- 240g all-purpose flour
- 50g granulated sugar
- 1 tbsp baking powder
- 1/4 tsp salt
- 115g unsalted butter, cold and cubed
- 180ml heavy cream, plus extra for brushing
- Whipped cream for serving
- Fresh mint leaves for garnish (optional)

## INSTRUCTION

1. Grease a baking dish that fits into Zone 1 of the air fryer.
2. Pour boiling water over chopped dates and let them sit for 10 minutes.
3. In a bowl, cream butter and brown sugar until light and fluffy. Add eggs one at a time, beating well after each addition. Stir in vanilla.
4. Sift flour, baking soda, and salt together, then add to the creamed mixture.
5. Fold in the softened dates and any remaining liquid.
6. Pour the batter into the greased baking dish.
7. Place the baking dish in Zone 1 of the air fryer.
8. Select Zone 1, choose the BAKE program, and set the temperature to 160°C. Set the time to 25-30 minutes. Press the START/STOP.
9. Meanwhile, prepare the toffee sauce by melting butter and sugar in a saucepan. Stir in double cream until smooth.
10. Check the pudding after 25 minutes. It should be firm to the touch and a toothpick should come out clean.
11. Once done, remove the baking dish from the air fryer and pierce the top with a skewer.
12. Pour half of the toffee sauce over the hot pudding, allowing it to soak in.
13. Serve the **Sticky Toffee Pudding** warm, drizzled with the remaining toffee sauce.

1. Combine sliced strawberries, 50g sugar, and lemon juice. Set aside.
2. In a bowl, whisk flour, 50g sugar, baking powder, and salt.
3. Cut cold butter into the flour mixture until it resembles coarse crumbs.
4. Gradually add heavy cream, mixing until dough just comes together.
5. Pat dough into a 2cm thick circle.
6. Cut out biscuits and place them on a baking tray or in the air fryer basket.
7. Brush biscuit tops with extra heavy cream.
8. Place the tray or basket in Zone 1 of the air fryer.
9. Select Zone 1, choose the BAKE program, and set the temperature to 180°C. Set the time to 10-12 minutes.
10. Check biscuits after 10 minutes. They should be golden brown.
11. Remove biscuits from the air fryer and let them cool slightly.
12. Split **biscuits** in half horizontally.
13. Spoon macerated strawberries over bottom halves. Top with whipped cream and the other biscuit half.
14. Garnish with fresh mint leaves if desired. Serve immediately.

# Tiramisu

🕐 **Cooking Time:** 25 Min  🍴 **Servings:** 8

- 3 large eggs, separated
- 75g granulated sugar
- 250g mascarpone cheese
- 150ml strong brewed coffee, cooled
- 30ml coffee liqueur (optional)
- 200g ladyfinger biscuits (savoiardi)
- Cocoa powder, for dusting

# Vanilla Custard Tart

🕐 **Cooking Time:** 30 Min  🍴 **Servings:** 8-10

- 250g shortcrust pastry (store-bought or homemade)
- 4 large eggs
- 100g caster sugar
- 2 tsp vanilla extract
- 300ml double cream
- Ground nutmeg, for sprinkling

## INSTRUCTION

1. In a bowl, beat the egg yolks with 50g of sugar until pale and creamy.
2. Add the mascarpone cheese to the egg yolk mixture and beat until smooth and well combined.
3. In a separate bowl, beat the egg whites with the remaining 25g of sugar until stiff peaks form.
4. Gently fold the beaten egg whites into the mascarpone mixture until fully incorporated. Set aside.
5. In a shallow dish, mix the cooled brewed coffee with the coffee liqueur (if using).
6. Dip each ladyfinger biscuit briefly into the coffee mixture, ensuring they are soaked but not soggy.
7. Arrange a layer of soaked ladyfinger biscuits in the bottom of a baking dish that fits into Zone 1 of the air fryer. Spread half of the mascarpone mixture over the layer of biscuits.
8. Repeat with another layer of soaked biscuits and the remaining mascarpone mixture.
9. Place the baking dish in Zone 1 of the air fryer. Select Zone 1, choose the BAKE program, and set the temperature to 160°C. Set the time to 20-25 minutes. Press the START/STOP.
10. Check the Tiramisu after 20 minutes. The top should be set and slightly firm to the touch.
11. Once done, carefully remove the baking dish from the air fryer and let the Tiramisu cool completely.
12. Dust the top of the Tiramisu with cocoa powder before serving.
13. Refrigerate the **Tiramisu** for at least 4 hours or overnight to set before serving.

1. Roll out the shortcrust pastry on a lightly floured surface to fit a tart tin that fits into Zone 1 of the air fryer.
2. Line the tart tin with the pastry, pressing it gently into the edges. Trim any excess pastry.
3. In a bowl, whisk together the eggs, caster sugar, and vanilla extract until well combined.
4. Gradually whisk in the double cream until smooth.
5. Pour the custard mixture into the pastry-lined tart tin.
6. Sprinkle the top of the custard with ground nutmeg.
7. Place the tart tin in Zone 1 of the air fryer.
8. Select Zone 1, choose the BAKE program, and set the temperature to 180°C. Set the time to 25-30 minutes.
9. Press the START/STOP button to begin cooking.
10. Check the custard tart after 25 minutes. The custard should be set around the edges but slightly wobbly in the center.
11. Once done, carefully remove the **tart** tin from the air fryer and let the custard tart cool completely.
12. Once cooled, refrigerate the custard tart for at least 1 hour before serving.

# Carrot Cake

⏱ **Cooking Time: 30 Min**   🍴 **Servings: 4**

- 200g self-raising flour
- 1 tsp baking powder
- 1 tsp ground cinnamon
- 1/2 tsp ground nutmeg
- 1/2 tsp ground ginger
- 150g light brown sugar
- 2 large eggs
- 150ml vegetable oil
- 200g grated carrots
- 50g chopped walnuts (optional)
- Cream cheese frosting (store-bought or homemade)

# Chocolate Lava Cake

⏱ **Cooking Time: 12 Min**   🍴 **Servings: 2-4**

- 115g dark chocolate, chopped
- 85g unsalted butter
- 50g granulated sugar
- 2 large eggs
- 1 tsp vanilla extract
- 30g all-purpose flour
- Pinch of salt
- Cocoa powder or powdered sugar, for dusting.

## INSTRUCTION

1. In a bowl, sift together the self-raising flour, baking powder, cinnamon, nutmeg, and ginger. Set aside.
2. In another bowl, whisk together the brown sugar and eggs until well combined.
3. Gradually add the vegetable oil to the egg mixture, whisking continuously.
4. Fold in the grated carrots and chopped walnuts (if using).
5. Gradually add the dry ingredients to the wet ingredients, mixing until just combined.
6. Grease a cake tin that fits into Zone 1 of the air fryer.
7. Pour the cake batter into the prepared tin, spreading it out evenly.
8. Place the cake tin in Zone 1 of the air fryer.
9. Select Zone 1, choose the BAKE program, and set the temperature to 160°C. Set the time to 25-30 minutes.
10. Press the START/STOP button to begin cooking.
11. Check the cake after 25 minutes. It should be golden brown and a toothpick inserted into the center should come out clean.
12. Once done, carefully remove the cake tin from the air fryer and let the cake cool completely.
13. Once cooled, spread cream cheese frosting over the top of the cake. Slice and serve the **Carrot Cake**.

1. In a microwave-safe bowl, combine the chopped dark chocolate and unsalted butter. Microwave in 30-second intervals, stirring between each interval, until melted and smooth. Set aside to cool slightly.
2. In a separate bowl, whisk together the granulated sugar, eggs, and vanilla extract until well combined.
3. Gradually pour the melted chocolate mixture into the egg mixture, whisking continuously.
4. Sift the all-purpose flour and salt into the chocolate mixture, then gently fold until just combined.
5. Grease ramekins or silicone muffin molds that fit into Zone 1 of the air fryer.
6. Divide the batter evenly among the prepared ramekins or molds.
7. Place the ramekins or molds in Zone 1 of the air fryer.
8. Select Zone 1, choose the BAKE program, and set the temperature to 180°C. Set the time to 10-12 minutes. Press the START/STOP.
9. Check the cakes after 10 minutes. The edges should be set, but the centers should still be soft.
10. Once done, carefully remove the ramekins or molds from the air fryer and let the cakes cool for a minute. Carefully invert the **cakes** onto serving plates. Dust with cocoa powder or powdered sugar before serving.

# Lemon Drizzle Cake

🕐 **Cooking Time:** 30 Min   🍴 **Servings:** 4-6

- 175g unsalted butter, softened
- 175g caster sugar
- 3 large eggs
- 175g self-raising flour
- Zest of 2 lemons
- Juice of 1 lemon
- 75g granulated sugar

# Bakewell Tart

🕐 **Cooking Time:** 30 Min   🍴 **Servings:** 4-6

- 250g shortcrust pastry (store-bought or homemade)
- 150g raspberry jam
- 125g unsalted butter, softened
- 125g caster sugar
- 2 large eggs
- 125g ground almonds
- 1/2 tsp almond extract
- 25g flaked almonds
- Icing sugar, for dusting

## INSTRUCTION

1. Grease a cake tin that fits into Zone 1 of the air fryer.
2. In a large bowl, cream together the softened butter and caster sugar until light and fluffy.
3. Beat in the eggs, one at a time, mixing well after each addition.
4. Sift the self-raising flour into the bowl and fold it into the mixture until well combined.
5. Stir in the lemon zest.
6. Pour the cake batter into the prepared tin, spreading it out evenly.
7. Place the cake tin in Zone 1 of the air fryer.
8. Select Zone 1, choose the BAKE program, and set the temperature to 160°C. Set the time to 25-30 minutes.
9. Press the START/STOP button to begin cooking.
10. While the cake is baking, mix the lemon juice with the granulated sugar to make the drizzle.
11. Once the cake is done, remove it from the air fryer and leave it in the tin.
12. While the cake is still warm, prick the surface all over with a skewer or fork.
13. Pour the lemon drizzle over the warm cake, allowing it to soak in.
14. Leave the **cake** to cool completely in the tin before removing and serving.

1. Roll out the shortcrust pastry on a lightly floured surface to fit a tart tin that fits into Zone 1 of the air fryer.
2. Line the tart tin with the pastry, pressing it gently into the edges. Trim any excess pastry.
3. Spread the raspberry jam evenly over the pastry base.
4. In a bowl, cream together the softened butter and caster sugar until light and fluffy.
5. Beat in the eggs, one at a time, mixing well after each addition.
6. Stir in the ground almonds and almond extract until well combined.
7. Spread the almond mixture over the raspberry jam in the tart case.
8. Sprinkle the flaked almonds over the top of the tart.
9. Place the tart tin in Zone 1 of the air fryer.
10. Select Zone 1, choose the BAKE program, and set the temperature to 180°C. Set the time to 25-30 minutes. Press the START/STOP.
11. Check the tart after 25 minutes. The almond mixture should be set and golden brown.
12. Once done, carefully remove the tart tin from the air fryer and let the **Bakewell Tart** cool completely.
13. Once cooled, dust the tart with icing sugar before serving

**Page 88**

# Crispy Air-Fried Potato Skins

🕐 **Cooking Time: 50 Min**　🍴 **Servings: 8 potato skins.**

- 4 large russet potatoes
- 2 tbsp olive oil
- Salt and pepper to taste
- 100g grated cheddar cheese
- 4 slices bacon, cooked and crumbled
- 2 spring onions, finely chopped
- Sour cream (optional), for serving

# Onion Rings

🕐 **Cooking Time: 12 Min**　🍴 **Servings: 4**

- 2 large onions, cut into rings
- 150g all-purpose flour
- 1 tsp baking powder
- 1/2 tsp salt
- 1/2 tsp paprika
- 1/4 tsp black pepper
- 180ml milk
- 1 large egg
- 100g breadcrumbs
- Cooking spray or oil mister

## INSTRUCTION

1. Scrub the potatoes clean and dry them with a paper towel.
2. Pierce each potato several times with a fork.
3. Rub the potatoes with olive oil and season them with salt and pepper.
4. Place the potatoes in Zone 1 of the air fryer. Select Zone 1, choose the AIR FRY program, and set the temperature to 200°C. Set the time to 35-40 minutes. Press the START/STOP.
5. Check the potatoes after 35 minutes. They should be tender when pierced with a fork.
6. Once the potatoes are cooked, carefully remove them from the air fryer and let them cool slightly.
7. Cut each potato in half lengthwise and scoop out the flesh, leaving about 0.6 cm of potato on the skin.
8. Evenly dividing potato skins between the two zone, Place them back in both Zone.
9. Select Zone 1, choose the AIR FRY program, and set the temperature to 200°C. Set the time to 8-10 minutes. Select MATCH. Press the START/STOP.
10. After 5 minutes, sprinkle the grated cheddar cheese and crumbled bacon evenly over the potato skins.
11. Continue cooking for another 3-5 minutes, or until the cheese is melted and bubbly.
12. Once done, carefully remove the potato skins from the air fryer and sprinkle them with chopped spring onions. Serve the **crispy potato skins** hot, with a dollop of sour cream if desired.

1. In a bowl, whisk together the flour, baking powder, salt, paprika, and black pepper.
2. In another bowl, whisk together the milk and egg.
3. Dip each onion ring into the flour mixture, then into the milk mixture, and finally into the breadcrumbs, coating evenly.
4. Place the coated onion rings in Zone 1 of the air fryer basket in a single layer, ensuring they are not touching.
5. Spray the onion rings with cooking spray or use an oil mister to lightly coat them.
6. Select Zone 1, choose the AIR FRY program, and set the temperature to 200°C. Set the time to 10-12 minutes.
7. Press the START/STOP button to begin cooking.
8. After 5 minutes, carefully flip the onion rings.
9. Continue cooking for another 5-7 minutes, or until the onion rings are golden brown and crispy.
10. Once done, carefully remove the onion rings from the air fryer and transfer them to a plate lined with paper towels to drain excess oil.
11. Serve the **crispy onion rings** immediately with your favorite dipping sauce.

# Buffalo Cauliflower Bites

🕐 **Cooking Time: 15 Min**   🍴 **Servings: 4**

- 1 head cauliflower, cut into florets
- 120g all-purpose flour
- 240ml milk (or plant-based milk for a vegan option)
- 1 tsp garlic powder
- 1/2 tsp salt
- 1/4 tsp black pepper
- 120ml buffalo hot sauce
- 60g unsalted butter (or vegan butter for a vegan option), melted
- Cooking spray or oil mister
- Ranch or blue cheese dressing for dipping (optional)
- Celery sticks (optional)

# Crispy Air-Fried Pickles

🕐 **Cooking Time: 10 Min**   🍴 **Servings: 20 pickle slices.**

- 240g dill pickle slices (about 20 slices)
- 120g all-purpose flour
- 2 large eggs
- 120g panko breadcrumbs
- 1/2 tsp garlic powder
- 1/2 tsp paprika
- 1/4 tsp cayenne pepper (optional)
- Cooking spray or oil mister
- Ranch or spicy mayo for dipping (optional)

## INSTRUCTION

1. In a bowl, whisk together the flour, milk, garlic powder, salt, and black pepper to make a batter.
2. Dip each cauliflower floret into the batter, ensuring it is evenly coated.
3. Shake off any excess batter and place the coated cauliflower florets in Zone 1 of the air fryer basket in a single layer, ensuring they are not touching.
4. Spray the cauliflower florets with cooking spray or use an oil mister to lightly coat them.
5. Select Zone 1, choose the AIR FRY program, and set the temperature to 200°C. Set the time to 12-15 minutes.
6. Press the START/STOP button to begin cooking.
7. While the cauliflower is cooking, mix the buffalo hot sauce and melted butter in a bowl.
8. After 6 minutes, carefully flip the cauliflower florets.
9. Continue cooking for another 6-9 minutes, or until the cauliflower is golden brown and crispy.
10. Once done, transfer the cooked cauliflower to a large bowl and pour the buffalo sauce mixture over the top. Toss until the cauliflower is evenly coated.
11. Serve the **Buffalo Cauliflower Bites** immediately with ranch or blue cheese dressing for dipping and celery sticks on the side.

1. Pat pickle slices dry with paper towels.
2. Set up a breading station with flour, beaten eggs, and a mixture of panko breadcrumbs, garlic powder, paprika, and cayenne pepper.
3. Dip pickle slices in flour, then eggs, then breadcrumb mixture.
4. Place breaded pickle slices in both Zone of the air fryer basket in a single layer.
5. Spray pickle slices with cooking spray or mist with oil.
6. Select Zone 1, choose the AIR FRY program, and set the temperature to 200°C for 8-10 minutes.
7. Select MATCH to duplicate settings across both zones. Press the START/STOP button to begin cooking.
8. After 4 minutes, carefully flip pickle slices.
9. Continue cooking for another 4-6 minutes until golden brown and crispy.
10. Remove **pickle slices** from air fryer and drain on paper towels.
11. Serve immediately with ranch or spicy mayo for dipping.

# Cheddar & Bacon Potato Bites

⏱ **Cooking Time:** 20 Min  🍴 **Servings:** 4

- 500g baby potatoes, halved
- 1 tbsp olive oil
- Salt and pepper to taste
- 100g grated cheddar cheese
- 4 slices bacon, cooked and crumbled
- 2 spring onions, finely chopped
- Sour cream (optional), for serving

# Sesame Chicken Wontons

⏱ **Cooking Time:** 10 Min  🍴 **Servings:** 20 wontons

- 200g ground chicken
- 1 spring onion, finely chopped
- 1/2 tsp grated ginger
- 1 clove garlic, minced
- 1 tbsp soy sauce
- 1 tsp sesame oil
- 1/2 tsp sugar
- 1/4 tsp salt
- 1/8 tsp black pepper
- 20 wonton wrappers
- 1 tbsp sesame seeds
- Cooking spray or oil mister
- Sweet chili sauce or soy sauce for dipping (optional)

## INSTRUCTION

1. In a bowl, toss the halved baby potatoes with olive oil, salt, and pepper until evenly coated.
2. Place the seasoned potatoes in both Zone of the air fryer basket in a single layer, ensuring they are not touching.
3. Select Zone 1, choose the AIR FRY program, and set the temperature to 200°C. Set the time to 18-20 minutes. Select MATCH to duplicate settings across both zones. Press the START/STOP.
4. After 10 minutes, carefully flip the potatoes for even cooking.
5. Continue cooking for another 8-10 minutes, or until the potatoes are golden brown and crispy.
6. Once done, remove the potatoes from the air fryer and transfer them to a bowl.
7. Add grated cheddar cheese and crumbled bacon to the bowl of hot potatoes and toss to melt the cheese.
8. Sprinkle with chopped spring onions.
9. Serve the **Cheddar and Bacon Potato Bites** hot, with a dollop of sour cream if desired.

1. In a bowl, mix together the ground chicken, spring onion, grated ginger, minced garlic, soy sauce, sesame oil, sugar, salt, and black pepper until well combined.
2. Place a small spoonful of the chicken mixture in the center of each wonton wrapper.
3. Moisten the edges of the wrapper with water, then fold it over the filling to form a triangle. Press the edges to seal.
4. Place the filled wontons in Zone 1 of the air fryer basket in a single layer, ensuring they are not touching.
5. Spray the wontons with cooking spray or mist with oil. Sprinkle sesame seeds over the wontons.
6. Select Zone 1, choose the AIR FRY program, and set the temperature to 180°C. Set the time to 8-10 minutes. Press the START/STOP.
7. After 4 minutes, carefully flip the wontons.
8. Continue cooking for another 4-6 minutes, or until the wontons are golden brown and crispy.
9. Once done, remove the wontons from the air fryer and transfer them to a plate.
10. Serve the **Sesame Chicken Wontons** hot, with sweet chili sauce or soy sauce for dipping if desired.

## Crispy Crab Rangoon

**Cooking Time:** 10 Min  **Servings:** 20 Crab Rangoon

- 120g cream cheese, softened
- 120g canned crab meat, drained
- 1 green onion, finely chopped
- 1/2 tsp Worcestershire sauce
- 1/4 tsp garlic powder
- 1/4 tsp onion powder
- Salt and pepper to taste
- 20 wonton wrappers
- Cooking spray or oil mister
- Sweet chili sauce for dipping (optional)

## Chickpea & Spinach Patties

**Cooking Time:** 15 Min  **Servings:** 6 patties

- 400g can chickpeas, drained and rinsed
- 100g fresh spinach, chopped
- 1 small onion, finely chopped
- 2 cloves garlic, minced
- 1 tsp ground cumin
- 1 tsp ground coriander
- 1/2 tsp paprika
- Salt and pepper to taste
- 1 tbsp lemon juice
- 2 tbsp all-purpose flour
- Cooking spray or oil mister.

## INSTRUCTION

1. In a bowl, mix together the softened cream cheese, crab meat, green onion, Worcestershire sauce, garlic powder, onion powder, salt, and pepper until well combined.
2. Place a small spoonful of the filling in the center of each wonton wrapper.
3. Moisten the edges of the wrapper with water, then fold it over the filling to form a triangle. Press the edges to seal.
4. Place the filled wontons in Zone 1 of the air fryer basket in a single layer, ensuring they are not touching.
5. Spray the wontons with cooking spray or mist with oil.
6. Select Zone 1, choose the AIR FRY program, and set the temperature to 180°C. Set the time to 8-10 minutes.
7. Press the START/STOP button to begin cooking.
8. After 4 minutes, carefully flip the wontons.
9. Continue cooking for another 4-6 minutes, or until the wontons are golden brown and crispy.
10. Once done, remove the wontons from the air fryer and transfer them to a plate.
11. Serve the **Crispy Crab Rangoon** hot, with sweet chili sauce for dipping if desired.

1. In a food processor, combine the chickpeas, spinach, onion, garlic, cumin, coriander, paprika, salt, pepper, and lemon juice. Pulse until well combined but still slightly chunky.
2. Transfer the mixture to a bowl and stir in the flour until the mixture holds together.
3. Shape the mixture into patties using your hands, compacting them firmly.
4. Place the patties in Zone 1 of the air fryer basket in a single layer, ensuring they are not touching.
5. Spray the patties with cooking spray or mist with oil.
6. Select Zone 1, choose the AIR FRY program, and set the temperature to 180°C. Set the time to 12-15 minutes.
7. Press the START/STOP button to begin cooking.
8. After 6 minutes, carefully flip the patties.
9. Continue cooking for another 6-9 minutes, or until the patties are golden brown and crispy.
10. Once done, remove the patties from the air fryer and transfer them to a plate.
11. Serve the **Chickpea and Spinach Patties** hot, with your favorite dipping sauce or in a bun as a burger.

## Breaded Avocado Slices

⏱ Cooking Time: 10 Min   🍴 Servings: 12 avocado slices

- 2 ripe avocados, pitted and sliced
- 120g all-purpose flour
- 2 large eggs, beaten
- 120g breadcrumbs
- 1/2 tsp garlic powder
- 1/2 tsp paprika
- 1/4 tsp cayenne pepper (optional)
- Salt and pepper to taste
- Cooking spray or oil mister
- Lime wedges for serving (optional)
- Chipotle mayo or ranch dressing for dipping (optional)

## Curry Puff Pastries

⏱ Cooking Time: 15 Min   🍴 Servings: 12 curry puff pastries

- 1 package of puff pastry sheets (thawed if frozen)
- 200g potatoes, peeled and diced
- 100g carrots, peeled and diced
- 1 onion, finely chopped
- 2 cloves garlic, minced
- 200g ground chicken or beef
- 2 tbsp curry powder
- 1 tsp ground turmeric
- Salt and pepper to taste
- 1 egg, beaten (for egg wash)
- Cooking spray or oil mister

## INSTRUCTION

1. In a shallow bowl, combine the breadcrumbs, garlic powder, paprika, cayenne pepper (if using), salt, and pepper.
2. Dredge each avocado slice in the flour, shaking off any excess.
3. Dip the floured avocado slice into the beaten eggs, allowing any excess to drip off.
4. Coat the avocado slice in the seasoned breadcrumb mixture, pressing gently to adhere.
5. Place the breaded avocado slices in Zone 1 of the air fryer basket in a single layer, ensuring they are not touching.
6. Spray the avocado slices with cooking spray or mist with oil.
7. Select Zone 1, choose the AIR FRY program, and set the temperature to 200°C. Set the time to 8-10 minutes.
8. Press the START/STOP button to begin cooking.
9. After 4 minutes, carefully flip the avocado slices.
10. Continue cooking for another 4-6 minutes, or until the avocado slices are golden brown and crispy.
11. Once done, remove the avocado slices from the air fryer and transfer them to a plate.
12. Serve the **Breaded Avocado Slices** hot, with lime wedges and chipotle mayo or ranch dressing for dipping if desired.

1. In a pan, heat a little oil over medium heat. Add the chopped onion and minced garlic, and cook until softened.
2. Add the ground chicken or beef to the pan and cook until browned.
3. Stir in the curry powder, ground turmeric, salt, and pepper. Cook for another minute. Add the diced potatoes and carrots to the pan. Cook until the vegetables are tender.
4. Roll out the puff pastry sheets and cut them into squares or rectangles, depending on your preference. Place a spoonful of the curry filling onto each pastry square.
5. Fold the pastry over the filling to form a triangle or rectangle, depending on the shape you cut. Use a fork to press down and seal the edges of the pastry.
6. Place the assembled curry puffs in both Zone of the air fryer basket in a single layer. Brush the tops of the curry puffs with beaten egg for a golden finish.
7. Select Zone 1, choose the AIR FRY program, set temperature to 180°C. Set time to 12-15 minutes. Select MATCH. Press the START/STOP.
8. After 6 minutes, carefully flip the curry puffs.
9. Continue cooking for another 6-9 minutes, or until the curry puffs are golden brown and crispy. Serve the **Curry Puff Pastries** hot as a delicious snack or appetizer.

# Crispy Air-Fried Okra

⏱ **Cooking Time:** 12 Min  🍴 **Servings:** 4

- 300g fresh okra, washed, dried, and sliced into 1/2-inch pieces
- 2 tbsp cornmeal
- 2 tbsp all-purpose flour
- 1/2 tsp garlic powder
- 1/2 tsp paprika
- 1/4 tsp cayenne pepper (optional)
- Salt and pepper to taste
- Cooking spray or oil mister
- Lemon wedges for serving (optional)
- Ranch dressing or hot sauce for dipping (optional)

# Garlic Herb Pita Chips

⏱ **Cooking Time:** 10 Min  🍴 **Servings:** 32 pita chips.

- 4 pita bread rounds
- 2 tbsp olive oil
- 1 tsp garlic powder
- 1 tsp dried mixed herbs (such as oregano, basil, thyme)
- Salt and pepper to taste

## INSTRUCTION

1. In a bowl, combine the cornmeal, flour, garlic powder, paprika, cayenne pepper (if using), salt, and pepper.
2. Add the sliced okra to the bowl and toss to coat evenly with the seasoned mixture.
3. Place the coated okra in Zone 1 of the air fryer basket in a single layer, ensuring they are not touching.
4. Spray the okra with cooking spray or mist with oil.
5. Select Zone 1, choose the AIR FRY program, and set the temperature to 200°C. Set the time to 10-12 minutes.
6. Press the START/STOP button to begin cooking.
7. After 5 minutes, carefully shake the basket or use tongs to flip the okra for even cooking.
8. Continue cooking for another 5-7 minutes, or until the okra is golden brown and crispy.
9. Once done, remove the okra from the air fryer and transfer it to a plate.
10. Serve the **Crispy Air-Fried Okra** hot, with lemon wedges and ranch dressing or hot sauce for dipping if desired.

1. Cut each pita bread round into 8 wedges.
2. In a bowl, mix together the olive oil, garlic powder, dried herbs, salt, and pepper.
3. Brush both sides of the pita wedges with the oil and herb mixture.
4. Place the coated pita wedges in both Zone of the air fryer basket in a single layer, ensuring they are not overlapping.
5. Select Zone 1, choose the AIR FRY program, and set the temperature to 180°C. Set the time to 6-8 minutes. Select MATCH to duplicate settings across both zones.
6. Press the START/STOP button to begin cooking.
7. After 3 minutes, carefully flip the pita wedges.
8. Continue cooking for another 3-5 minutes, or until the pita chips are golden brown and crispy.
9. Once done, remove the pita chips from the air fryer and transfer them to a plate to cool.
10. Serve the **Garlic Herb Pita Chips** as a delicious snack or with your favorite dips.

## Crispy Cauliflower Wings

⏱ **Cooking Time:** 18 Min  🍴 **Servings:** 4

- 1 head cauliflower, cut into florets
- 120g all-purpose flour
- 240ml milk (or plant-based milk)
- 1 tsp garlic powder
- 1 tsp paprika
- 1/2 tsp cumin
- 1/2 tsp salt
- 1/4 tsp black pepper
- Cooking spray or oil mister
- 120ml buffalo hot sauce
- 60g unsalted butter, melted
- Ranch or blue cheese dressing for dipping (optional)
- Celery sticks (optional)

## Prawn Toast

⏱ **Cooking Time:** 10 Min  🍴 **Servings:** 8 pieces of prawn toast

- 200g raw prawns, peeled and deveined
- 2 slices white bread, crusts removed
- 1 egg white
- 1 tsp soy sauce
- 1/2 tsp sesame oil
- 1/2 tsp sugar
- 1/4 tsp salt
- 1/4 tsp white pepper
- 2 spring onions, finely chopped
- Cooking spray or oil mister
- Sweet chili sauce for dipping (optional)

## INSTRUCTION

1. In a bowl, whisk together the flour, milk, garlic powder, paprika, cumin, salt, and black pepper until smooth.
2. Dip each cauliflower floret into the batter, ensuring it is evenly coated.
3. Shake off any excess batter and place the coated cauliflower florets in Zone 1 of the air fryer basket in a single layer.
4. Spray the cauliflower florets with cooking spray or use an oil mister to lightly coat them.
5. Select Zone 1, choose the AIR FRY program, and set the temperature to 200°C. Set the time to 15-18 minutes.
6. Press the START/STOP button to begin cooking.
7. After 8 minutes, carefully flip the cauliflower florets.
8. Continue cooking for another 7-10 minutes, or until the cauliflower is golden brown and crispy.
9. While the cauliflower is cooking, mix the buffalo hot sauce and melted butter in a bowl.
10. Once done, transfer the cooked cauliflower to a large bowl and pour the buffalo sauce mixture over the top. Toss until the cauliflower is evenly coated.
11. Serve the **Crispy Cauliflower Wings** immediately with ranch or blue cheese dressing for dipping and celery sticks on the side.

1. In a food processor, blend the raw prawns until they form a paste.
2. Cut the bread slices into quarters to make smaller squares.
3. In a bowl, combine the prawn paste, egg white, soy sauce, sesame oil, sugar, salt, white pepper, and chopped spring onions.
4. Spread a generous amount of the prawn mixture onto each bread square, covering the surface evenly.
5. Place the prawn toast in Zone 1 of the air fryer basket in a single layer, ensuring they are not touching.
6. Spray the prawn toast with cooking spray or mist with oil.
7. Select Zone 1, choose the AIR FRY program, and set the temperature to 180°C. Set the time to 8-10 minutes. Press the START/STOP button to begin cooking.
8. After 4 minutes, carefully flip the prawn toast.
9. Continue cooking for another 4-6 minutes, or until the prawn toast is golden brown and crispy.
10. Once done, remove the prawn toast from the air fryer and transfer them to a plate.
11. Serve the **Prawn Toast** hot, with sweet chili sauce for dipping if desired.

## Samosas

🕐 **Cooking Time:** 15 Min  🍴 **Servings:** 12 samosas.

- 2 large potatoes, peeled and diced
- 100g frozen peas
- 1 small onion, finely chopped
- 2 cloves garlic, minced
- 1 tsp grated ginger
- 1 green chili, finely chopped (optional)
- 1 tsp ground cumin
- 1 tsp ground coriander
- 1/2 tsp turmeric
- 1/2 tsp garam masala
- Salt to taste
- 2 tbsp vegetable oil
- 12 samosa wrappers or phyllo pastry sheets
- Cooking spray or oil mister

## Mozzarella Sticks

🕐 **Cooking Time:** 10 Min  🍴 **Servings:** 24 mozzarella sticks

- 12 mozzarella cheese sticks
- 120g all-purpose flour
- 2 large eggs, beaten
- 120g breadcrumbs
- 1/2 tsp garlic powder
- 1/2 tsp dried oregano
- 1/2 tsp dried basil
- 1/4 tsp cayenne pepper (optional)
- Salt and pepper to taste
- Cooking spray or oil mister
- Marinara sauce for dipping

---

## INSTRUCTION

1. Boil the diced potatoes and frozen peas until tender. Drain and set aside.
2. In a pan, heat the vegetable oil over medium heat. Add the chopped onion and cook until translucent.
3. Add the minced garlic, grated ginger, and green chili (if using) to the pan. Cook for another minute.
4. Stir in the ground cumin, ground coriander, turmeric, garam masala, and salt. Cook for a few minutes until fragrant.
5. Add the boiled potatoes and peas to the pan. Mix well and cook for another 5 minutes. Remove from heat and let the mixture cool.
6. Once the potato mixture has cooled, place a spoonful of the filling onto each samosa wrapper.
7. Fold the wrapper over the filling to form a triangle. Seal the edges using a little water.
8. Place the assembled samosas in both Zone of the air fryer basket in a single layer, ensuring they are not touching.
9. Spray the samosas with cooking spray or mist with oil.
10. AIR FRY at 180°C for 12-15 minutes, (Select MATCH) flipping halfway through, until golden brown and crispy.
11. Once done, remove the **samosas** from the air fryer and serve hot with chutney.

---

1. Cut the mozzarella cheese sticks in half to make 24 shorter sticks.
2. In three separate shallow dishes, place the flour in one, beaten eggs in another, and breadcrumbs mixed with garlic powder, dried oregano, dried basil, cayenne pepper (if using), salt, and pepper in the third.
3. Dredge each mozzarella stick in the flour, then dip it into the beaten eggs, and finally coat it with the breadcrumb mixture, pressing gently to adhere.
4. Place the coated mozzarella sticks in both Zone of the air fryer basket in a single layer, ensuring they are not touching.
5. Spray the mozzarella sticks with cooking spray or mist with oil.
6. Select Zone 1, choose the AIR FRY program, and set the temperature to 180°C. Set the time to 6-8 minutes. Select MATCH. Press the START/STOP.
7. After 3 minutes, carefully flip the mozzarella sticks.
8. Continue cooking for another 3-5 minutes, or until the mozzarella sticks are golden brown and crispy.
9. Once done, remove the mozzarella sticks from the air fryer and transfer them to a plate.
10. Serve the **Mozzarella Sticks** hot, with marinara sauce for dipping.

# Jalapeño Poppers

🕐 **Cooking Time:** 10 Min   🍴 **Servings:** 24 jalapeño poppers

- 12 jalapeño peppers, halved lengthwise and seeded
- 200g cream cheese, softened
- 100g cheddar cheese, shredded
- 1/2 tsp garlic powder
- 1/2 tsp onion powder
- Salt and pepper to taste
- 120g all-purpose flour
- 2 large eggs, beaten
- 120g breadcrumbs
- Cooking spray or oil mister
- Ranch dressing or sour cream for dipping

# Mini Pizzas

🕐 **Cooking Time:** 10 Min   🍴 **Servings:** 8 mini pizzas

- 4 English muffins, split
- 200g pizza sauce
- 200g mozzarella cheese, shredded
- Your choice of toppings (e.g., pepperoni, sliced bell peppers, sliced mushrooms, etc.)
- Fresh basil leaves (optional)
- Cooking spray or oil mister

---

## INSTRUCTION

---

1. In a bowl, mix together the softened cream cheese, shredded cheddar cheese, garlic powder, onion powder, salt, and pepper until well combined.
2. Fill each jalapeño half with the cream cheese mixture, pressing gently to fill.
3. Place the filled jalapeño halves in both Zone of the air fryer basket in a single layer, ensuring they are not touching.
4. Set up a breading station with three shallow dishes: one with flour, one with beaten eggs, and one with breadcrumbs.
5. Dredge each stuffed jalapeño half in the flour, then dip it into the beaten eggs, and finally coat it with breadcrumbs, pressing gently to adhere.
6. Place the coated jalapeño poppers back in both Zone of the air fryer basket.
7. Spray the jalapeño poppers with cooking spray or mist with oil.
8. Select Zone 1, choose the AIR FRY program, and set the temperature to 180°C. Set the time to 8-10 minutes. Select MATCH. Press the START/STOP button to begin cooking.
9. After 4 minutes, carefully flip the jalapeño poppers.
10. Continue cooking for another 4-6 minutes, or until the jalapeño poppers are golden brown and crispy.
11. Serve the **Jalapeño Poppers** hot, with ranch dressing or sour cream for dipping.

1. Place the English muffin halves on a clean surface or cutting board.
2. Spread a spoonful of pizza sauce on each English muffin half, covering the surface evenly.
3. Sprinkle a generous amount of shredded mozzarella cheese over the sauce on each muffin half.
4. Add your choice of toppings on top of the cheese.
5. Place the assembled mini pizzas in Zone 1 of the air fryer basket in a single layer, ensuring they are not touching.
6. Spray the mini pizzas with cooking spray or mist with oil.
7. Select Zone 1, choose the AIR FRY program, and set the temperature to 180°C. Set the time to 8-10 minutes. Select MATCH to duplicate settings across both zones. Press the START/STOP button to begin cooking.
8. After 4 minutes, carefully check the mini pizzas to see if the cheese is melted and the crust is golden brown. If not, continue cooking for another 4-6 minutes.
9. Once done, remove the mini pizzas from the air fryer and transfer them to a plate.
10. Garnish with fresh basil leaves if desired. Serve the **Mini Pizzas** hot as a delicious snack or meal

## Croutons

⏱ **Cooking Time: 7 Min**  🍴 **Servings: 4**

- 4 slices of bread (white or wholemeal), cut into cubes
- 2 tbsp olive oil
- 1/2 tsp garlic powder
- 1/2 tsp dried thyme
- Salt and pepper to taste

## Falafel

⏱ **Cooking Time: 15 Min**  🍴 **Servings: 12-15 falafel**

- 240g dried chickpeas, soaked overnight
- 1 small onion, roughly chopped
- 3 cloves garlic, minced
- 1 handful fresh parsley, chopped
- 1 handful fresh coriander, chopped
- 1 tsp ground cumin
- 1 tsp ground coriander
- 1/2 tsp baking soda
- Salt and pepper to taste
- Cooking spray or oil mister

## INSTRUCTION

1. In a bowl, toss the bread cubes with olive oil, garlic powder, dried thyme, salt, and pepper until evenly coated.
2. Place the seasoned bread cubes in Zone 1 of the air fryer basket in a single layer, ensuring they are not overcrowded.
3. Select Zone 1, choose the AIR FRY program, and set the temperature to 180°C. Set the time to 5-7 minutes.
4. Press the START/STOP button to begin cooking.
5. After 3 minutes, open the air fryer and shake the basket to ensure even cooking.
6. Continue cooking for another 2-4 minutes, or until the croutons are golden brown and crispy.
7. Once done, remove the croutons from the air fryer and let them cool before using or storing.
8. Store the **croutons** in an airtight container once cooled.

1. Drain the soaked chickpeas and pat them dry with a paper towel.
2. In a food processor, combine the chickpeas, onion, garlic, parsley, coriander, ground cumin, ground coriander, baking soda, salt, and pepper. Pulse until the mixture is coarse but not pureed.
3. Form the mixture into small balls or patties, about the size of a golf ball.
4. Place the formed falafel in Zone 1 of the air fryer basket in a single layer, ensuring they are not touching.
5. Spray the falafel with cooking spray or mist with oil.
6. Select Zone 1, choose the AIR FRY program, and set the temperature to 200°C. Set the time to 12-15 minutes.
7. Press the START/STOP button to begin cooking.
8. After 6 minutes, carefully flip the falafel.
9. Continue cooking for another 6-9 minutes, or until the falafel are golden brown and crispy.
10. Once done, remove the falafel from the air fryer and let them cool for a few minutes before serving.
11. Serve the **Falafel** with pita bread, salad, and your choice of sauce or dressing.

# Crispy Tofu Bites

🕐 **Cooking Time:** 15 Min  🍴 **Servings:** 4

- 350g extra-firm tofu, drained and pressed
- 2 tbsp cornstarch
- 1/2 tsp garlic powder
- 1/2 tsp smoked paprika
- 1/4 tsp salt
- 1/4 tsp black pepper
- Cooking spray or oil mister.

# Vegetarian Burger Patties

🕐 **Cooking Time:** 15 Min  🍴 **Servings:** 4 vegetarian burger patties

- 400g canned chickpeas, drained and rinsed
- 1 small onion, finely chopped
- 2 cloves garlic, minced
- 1 carrot, grated
- 1 small red bell pepper, finely chopped
- 60g rolled oats
- 2 tbsp tomato paste
- 1 tsp ground cumin
- 1 tsp smoked paprika
- 1/2 tsp ground coriander
- Salt and pepper to taste
- Cooking spray or oil mister

## INSTRUCTION

**Crispy Tofu Bites:**

1. Cut the pressed tofu into bite-sized cubes.
2. In a bowl, combine the cornstarch, garlic powder, smoked paprika, salt, and black pepper.
3. Toss the tofu cubes in the cornstarch mixture until evenly coated.
4. Place the coated tofu cubes in Zone 1 of the air fryer basket in a single layer, ensuring they are not touching.
5. Spray the tofu cubes with cooking spray or mist with oil.
6. Select Zone 1, choose the AIR FRY program, and set the temperature to 200°C. Set the time to 12-15 minutes.
7. Press the START/STOP button to begin cooking.
8. After 6 minutes, carefully flip the tofu cubes.
9. Continue cooking for another 6-9 minutes, or until the tofu bites are golden brown and crispy.
10. Once done, remove the crispy tofu bites from the air fryer and let them cool for a few minutes before serving.
11. Serve the **Crispy Tofu Bites** with your favorite dipping sauce or use them in salads, wraps, or bowls.

**Vegetarian Burger Patties:**

1. In a food processor, pulse the chickpeas until coarsely chopped.
2. Transfer the chopped chickpeas to a mixing bowl and add the chopped onion, minced garlic, grated carrot, chopped red bell pepper, rolled oats, tomato paste, ground cumin, smoked paprika, ground coriander, salt, and pepper. Mix until well combined.
3. Divide the mixture into 4 equal portions and shape each portion into a patty.
4. Place the patties in Zone 1 of the air fryer basket in a single layer, ensuring they are not touching.
5. Spray the patties with cooking spray or mist with oil.
6. Select Zone 1, choose the AIR FRY program, and set the temperature to 200°C. Set the time to 15-18 minutes. Press the START/STOP button to begin cooking.
7. After 8 minutes, carefully flip the patties.
8. Continue cooking for another 7-10 minutes, or until the patties are golden brown and crispy on the outside.
9. Once done, remove the vegetarian burger patties from the air fryer and let them cool for a few minutes before serving. Serve the **Vegetarian Burger Patties** on buns with your favorite toppings and condiments.

# Super Vegetable Burger

**Cooking Time:** 25 Min  **Servings:** 4

- 400g canned chickpeas, drained and rinsed
- 1 small onion, finely chopped
- 2 cloves garlic, minced
- 1 carrot, grated
- 1 small red bell pepper, finely chopped
- 60g rolled oats
- 2 tbsp tomato paste
- 1 tsp ground cumin
- 1 tsp smoked paprika
- 1/2 tsp ground coriander
- Salt and pepper to taste
- 4 wholemeal burger buns
- Lettuce leaves
- Sliced tomatoes
- Sliced red onion
- Sliced avocado

# Vegetarian Sausages

**Cooking Time:** 15 Min  **Servings:** 8 Vegetarian Sausages.

- 200g cooked and cooled quinoa
- 200g cooked and cooled lentils
- 1 small onion, finely chopped
- 2 cloves garlic, minced
- 2 tbsp tomato paste
- 1 tsp smoked paprika
- 1/2 tsp dried thyme
- 1/2 tsp dried sage
- Salt and pepper to taste
- 2 tbsp olive oil
- 60g breadcrumbs
- Cooking spray or oil mister.

## INSTRUCTION

1. In a food processor, pulse the chickpeas until coarsely chopped.
2. Transfer the chopped chickpeas to a mixing bowl and add the chopped onion, minced garlic, grated carrot, chopped red bell pepper, rolled oats, tomato paste, ground cumin, smoked paprika, ground coriander, salt, and pepper. Mix until well combined.
3. Divide the mixture into 4 equal portions and shape each portion into a patty.
4. Place the patties in Zone 1 of the air fryer basket in a single layer, spray the patties with cooking spray or mist with oil.
5. Select Zone 1, choose the AIR FRY program, and set the temperature to 200°C. Set the time to 15-18 minutes. Press the START/STOP.
6. After 8 minutes, carefully flip the patties. Continue cooking for another 7-10 minutes, or until the patties are golden brown and crispy on the outside.
7. Once done, remove the vegetarian burger patties from the air fryer and let them cool for a few minutes.
8. Toast the burger buns in the air fryer for 2-3 minutes.
9. Assemble the **Super Vegetable Burgers** by placing a patty on each bun, topping with lettuce, tomato slices, red onion slices, avocado slices, and your favorite burger sauce or condiments.

1. In a large bowl, mash the cooked quinoa and lentils together using a fork or potato masher until well combined.
2. Add the chopped onion, minced garlic, tomato paste, smoked paprika, dried thyme, dried sage, salt, pepper, and olive oil to the bowl. Mix until everything is evenly distributed.
3. Gradually add the breadcrumbs to the mixture, stirring well until it reaches a firm consistency that can be shaped into sausages.
4. Divide the mixture into 8 equal portions and shape each portion into a sausage shape.
5. Place the sausages in Zone 1 of the air fryer basket in a single layer, ensuring they are not touching.
6. Spray the sausages with cooking spray or mist with oil.
7. Select Zone 1, choose the AIR FRY program, and set the temperature to 180°C. Set the time to 12-15 minutes. Press the START/STOP.
8. After 6 minutes, carefully flip the sausages. Continue cooking for another 6-9 minutes, or until the sausages are golden brown and crispy.
9. Serve the **Vegetarian Sausages** with your favorite sides or use them in sandwiches or wraps.

# Zucchini Fritters

⏱ **Cooking Time:** 12 Min  🍴 **Servings:** 8 Zucchini Fritters.

- 2 medium zucchinis, grated
- 1 small onion, grated
- 2 cloves garlic, minced
- 2 eggs, beaten
- 60g breadcrumbs
- 30g grated Parmesan cheese
- 1/2 tsp dried oregano
- 1/2 tsp dried basil
- Salt and pepper to taste
- Cooking spray or oil mister

# Cauliflower Wings

⏱ **Cooking Time:** 20 Min  🍴 **Servings:** 4

- 1 medium head cauliflower, cut into florets
- 120g all-purpose flour
- 240ml unsweetened plant-based milk
- 1 tsp garlic powder
- 1 tsp onion powder
- 1/2 tsp smoked paprika
- Salt and pepper to taste
- Cooking spray or oil mister
- Your favorite wing sauce (e.g., buffalo sauce, barbecue sauce)

## INSTRUCTION

1. Place the grated zucchini in a clean kitchen towel or cheesecloth and squeeze out excess moisture.
2. In a large bowl, combine the grated zucchini, grated onion, minced garlic, beaten eggs, breadcrumbs, grated Parmesan cheese, dried oregano, dried basil, salt, and pepper. Mix until well combined.
3. Divide the mixture into 8 equal portions and shape each portion into a fritter.
4. Place the fritters in Zone 1 of the air fryer basket in a single layer, ensuring they are not touching.
5. Spray the fritters with cooking spray or mist with oil.
6. Select Zone 1, choose the AIR FRY program, and set the temperature to 180°C. Set the time to 10-12 minutes.
7. Press the START/STOP button to begin cooking.
8. After 5 minutes, carefully flip the fritters.
9. Continue cooking for another 5-7 minutes, or until the fritters are golden brown and crispy.
10. Once done, remove the zucchini fritters from the air fryer and let them cool for a few minutes before serving.
11. Serve the **Zucchini Fritters** with a side of yogurt sauce or your favorite dipping sauce.

1. In a large bowl, whisk together the all-purpose flour, plant-based milk, garlic powder, onion powder, smoked paprika, salt, and pepper to make a smooth batter.
2. Dip each cauliflower floret into the batter, coating it completely, and shake off any excess.
3. Place the coated cauliflower florets in Zone 1 of the air fryer basket in a single layer, ensuring they are not touching.
4. Spray the cauliflower florets with cooking spray or mist with oil.
5. Select Zone 1, choose the AIR FRY program, and set the temperature to 200°C. Set the time to 15-18 minutes.
6. Press the START/STOP button to begin cooking.
7. After 8 minutes, carefully flip the cauliflower florets.
8. Continue cooking for another 7-10 minutes, or until the cauliflower is golden brown and crispy.
9. Once done, remove the cauliflower wings from the air fryer and let them cool for a few minutes.
10. Toss the cauliflower wings in your favorite wing sauce until evenly coated.
11. Serve the **Cauliflower Wings** hot as a delicious appetizer or snack

## Aloo Tikki

⏱ **Cooking Time:** 20 Min  🍴 **Servings:** 8 Aloo Tikkis

- 4 medium potatoes, boiled, peeled, and mashed
- 1 small onion, finely chopped
- 2 green chilies, finely chopped
- 1/2 tsp cumin seeds
- 1/2 tsp garam masala
- 1/2 tsp red chili powder
- 1/2 tsp chaat masala
- 2 tbsp chopped coriander leaves
- Salt to taste
- 2 tbsp breadcrumbs
- Cooking spray or oil mister

## Vegan Nuggets

⏱ **Cooking Time:** 20 Min  🍴 **Servings:** 12-15 Vegan Nuggets

- 200g canned chickpeas, drained and rinsed
- 100g cooked quinoa
- 50g breadcrumbs
- 1 tbsp nutritional yeast
- 1 tsp onion powder
- 1 tsp garlic powder
- 1/2 tsp smoked paprika
- Salt and pepper to taste
- Cooking spray or oil mister

## INSTRUCTION

1. In a bowl, combine the mashed potatoes, chopped onion, green chilies, cumin seeds, garam masala, red chili powder, chaat masala, chopped coriander leaves, and salt. Mix well.
2. Divide the mixture into 8 equal portions and shape each portion into a flat round patty (tikki).
3. Coat each tikki with breadcrumbs on both sides.
4. Place the tikkis in Zone 1 of the air fryer basket in a single layer, ensuring they are not touching.
5. Spray the tikkis with cooking spray or mist with oil.
6. Select Zone 1, choose the AIR FRY program, and set the temperature to 200°C. Set the time to 15-18 minutes.
7. Press the START/STOP button to begin cooking.
8. After 8 minutes, carefully flip the tikkis.
9. Continue cooking for another 7-10 minutes, or until the tikkis are golden brown and crispy.
10. Once done, remove the Aloo Tikkis from the air fryer and let them cool for a few minutes.
11. Serve the **Aloo Tikkis** hot with chutney or sauce of your choice.

1. In a food processor, combine the chickpeas, cooked quinoa, breadcrumbs, nutritional yeast, onion powder, garlic powder, smoked paprika, salt, and pepper. Pulse until the mixture comes together but still has some texture.
2. Using your hands, shape the mixture into small nugget-sized pieces.
3. Place the nuggets in Zone 1 of the air fryer basket, ensuring they are not touching.
4. Spray the nuggets with cooking spray or mist with oil.
5. Select Zone 1, choose the AIR FRY program, and set the temperature to 200°C. Set the time to 15-18 minutes.
6. Press the START/STOP button to begin cooking.
7. After 8 minutes, carefully flip the nuggets.
8. Continue cooking for another 7-10 minutes, or until the nuggets are golden brown and crispy.
9. Once done, remove the Vegan Nuggets from the air fryer and let them cool for a few minutes.
10. Serve the **Vegan Nuggets** hot with your favorite dipping sauce or as a snack or meal.

# Vegetable Tempura

🕐 **Cooking Time:** 10 Min  🍴 **Servings:** 4

- Assorted vegetables (e.g., bell peppers, sweet potatoes, zucchini, mushrooms), sliced into bite-sized pieces
- 120g all-purpose flour
- 1/2 tsp baking powder
- 1/2 tsp salt
- 240 ml ice-cold sparkling water
- Cooking spray or oil mister
- Tempura dipping sauce or soy sauce for serving

# Vegetable Stir-Fry

🕐 **Cooking Time:** 10 Min  🍴 **Servings:** 4

- 1 tbsp vegetable oil
- 1 onion, sliced
- 2 cloves garlic, minced
- 1 bell pepper, sliced
- 1 carrot, julienned
- 100g broccoli florets
- 100g snap peas
- 100g mushrooms, sliced
- 2 tbsp soy sauce
- 1 tbsp vegan oyster sauce
- 1 tsp sesame oil
- Salt and pepper to taste
- Cooked rice or noodles for serving

## INSTRUCTION

1. In a bowl, whisk together the all-purpose flour, baking powder, and salt.
2. Gradually add the ice-cold sparkling water to the flour mixture, whisking until smooth. The batter should be thin and slightly lumpy.
3. Dip the assorted vegetables into the batter, coating them evenly.
4. Place the coated vegetables in Zone 1 of the air fryer basket in a single layer, ensuring they are not touching.
5. Spray the vegetables with cooking spray or mist with oil.
6. Select Zone 1, choose the AIR FRY program, and set the temperature to 200°C. Set the time to 8-10 minutes.
7. Press the START/STOP button to begin cooking.
8. After 4 minutes, carefully flip the vegetables.
9. Continue cooking for another 4-6 minutes, or until the tempura is golden brown and crispy.
10. Once done, remove the Vegetable Tempura from the air fryer and let them cool for a few minutes.
11. Serve the **Vegetable Tempura** hot with tempura dipping sauce or soy sauce.

1. In a large pan or wok, heat the vegetable oil over medium-high heat.
2. Add the sliced onion and minced garlic to the pan. Stir-fry for 1-2 minutes until fragrant. Add the bell pepper, julienned carrot, broccoli florets, snap peas, and sliced mushrooms to the pan. Stir-fry for 4-5 minutes until the vegetables are tender-crisp.
3. In a small bowl, mix together the soy sauce, oyster sauce (if using), and sesame oil.
4. Pour the sauce mixture over the vegetables in the pan. Stir-fry for another 1-2 minutes to coat the vegetables evenly with the sauce. Season with salt and pepper to taste.
5. Transfer the stir-fried vegetables to the Ninja Dual Zone Air Fryer basket.
6. Select Zone 1, choose the AIR FRY program, and set the temperature to 200°C. Set the time to 8-10 minutes.
7. Press the START/STOP button to begin cooking.
8. After 4 minutes, carefully toss the vegetables in the basket.
9. Continue cooking for another 4-6 minutes, or until the vegetables are slightly charred and tender.
10. Once done, remove the **Vegetable Stir-Fry** from the air fryer and serve hot over cooked rice or noodles.

## Stuffed Bell Peppers

⏱ **Cooking Time:** 25 Min  🍴 **Servings:** 4

- 4 large bell peppers (any color), tops removed and seeds removed
- 200g cooked quinoa
- 1 can (400g) black beans, drained and rinsed
- 200g corn kernels
- 1 small onion, finely chopped
- 2 cloves garlic, minced
- 1 tsp ground cumin
- 1 tsp chili powder
- 1/2 tsp smoked paprika
- Salt and pepper to taste
- 100g shredded cheese (optional, for topping)
- Fresh cilantro, chopped (for garnish)
- Cooking spray or oil mister

## Mushroom Skewers

⏱ **Cooking Time:** 12 Min  🍴 **Servings:** 4

- 250g button mushrooms, cleaned and stems removed
- 1 bell pepper, cut into chunks
- 1 red onion, cut into chunks
- 2 tbsp olive oil
- 2 cloves garlic, minced
- 1 tsp dried thyme
- 1 tsp dried rosemary
- Salt and pepper to taste
- Wooden skewers, soaked in water for 30 minutes

## INSTRUCTION

1. In a large bowl, mix together the cooked quinoa, black beans, corn kernels, chopped onion, minced garlic, ground cumin, chili powder, smoked paprika, salt, and pepper.
2. Stuff each bell pepper with the quinoa and black bean mixture, pressing down gently to fill them.
3. Place the stuffed bell peppers in Zone 1 of the air fryer basket, standing upright.
4. Spray the tops of the stuffed bell peppers with cooking spray or mist with oil.
5. Select Zone 1, choose the AIR FRY program, and set the temperature to 180°C. Set the time to 20-25 minutes.
6. Press the START/STOP button to begin cooking.
7. After 15 minutes, sprinkle the shredded cheese on top of each stuffed bell pepper (if using).
8. Continue cooking for another 5-10 minutes, or until the bell peppers are tender and the cheese is melted and bubbly.
9. Once done, remove the **stuffed bell peppers** from the air fryer and let them cool for a few minutes.
10. Garnish with chopped fresh cilantro before serving.

1. In a bowl, combine the olive oil, minced garlic, dried thyme, dried rosemary, salt, and pepper.
2. Add the mushrooms, bell pepper chunks, and red onion chunks to the bowl. Toss to coat the vegetables evenly with the oil and seasoning mixture.
3. Thread the marinated mushrooms, bell pepper, and red onion onto the soaked wooden skewers, alternating between the vegetables.
4. Place the assembled skewers in Zone 1 of the air fryer basket, ensuring they are not touching.
5. Select Zone 1, choose the AIR FRY program, and set the temperature to 200°C. Set the time to 10-12 minutes.
6. Press the START/STOP button to begin cooking.
7. After 5 minutes, carefully flip the skewers.
8. Continue cooking for another 5-7 minutes, or until the vegetables are tender and slightly charred.
9. Once done, remove the Mushroom Skewers from the air fryer and let them cool for a few minutes.
10. Serve the **Mushroom Skewers** hot as a delicious appetizer or side dish.

# Vegetarian Kebabs

🕐 **Cooking Time: 12 Min**   🍴 **Servings: 4**

- 200g paneer, cut into cubes
- 1 bell pepper, cut into chunks
- 1 red onion, cut into chunks
- 1 zucchini, sliced
- 150 g - 200 g cherry tomatoes
- 2 tbsp olive oil
- 2 cloves garlic, minced
- 1 tsp dried oregano
- 1 tsp dried basil
- Salt and pepper to taste
- Wooden skewers, soaked in water for 30 minutes

# Veggie Fritters

🕐 **Cooking Time: 15 Min**   🍴 **Servings: 8-10 Veggie Fritters.**

- 2 medium zucchinis, grated (about 300g)
- 1 medium carrot, grated (about 150g)
- 100g corn kernels
- 25g chopped fresh parsley
- 25g chopped fresh coriander
- 60g all-purpose flour
- 25g grated Parmesan cheese
- 2 eggs, beaten
- 1/2 tsp baking powder
- Salt and pepper to taste
- Cooking spray or oil mister

## INSTRUCTION

1. In a bowl, combine the olive oil, minced garlic, dried oregano, dried basil, salt, and pepper.
2. Add the paneer cubes, bell pepper chunks, red onion chunks, zucchini slices, and cherry tomatoes to the bowl. Toss to coat the vegetables and paneer evenly with the oil and seasoning mixture.
3. Thread the marinated paneer and vegetables onto the soaked wooden skewers, alternating between them.
4. Place the assembled skewers in Zone 1 of the air fryer basket, ensuring they are not touching.
5. Select Zone 1, choose the AIR FRY program, and set the temperature to 200°C. Set the time to 10-12 minutes.
6. Press the START/STOP button to begin cooking.
7. After 5 minutes, carefully flip the skewers.
8. Continue cooking for another 5-7 minutes, or until the vegetables are tender and the paneer is golden brown.
9. Once done, remove the Vegetarian Kebabs from the air fryer and let them cool for a few minutes.
10. Serve the **Vegetarian Kebabs** hot as a delicious appetizer or main dish.

1. Place the grated zucchini and carrot in a clean kitchen towel and squeeze out excess moisture.
2. In a large bowl, combine the grated zucchini, grated carrot, corn kernels, chopped parsley, chopped coriander, all-purpose flour, grated Parmesan cheese, beaten eggs, baking powder, salt, and pepper. Mix until well combined.
3. Line the air fryer basket with parchment paper or lightly grease it with cooking spray.
4. Using a spoon or your hands, scoop out portions of the vegetable mixture and shape them into fritters.
5. Place the fritters in Zone 1 of the air fryer basket, ensuring they are not touching.
6. Spray the fritters with cooking spray or mist with oil.
7. Select Zone 1, choose the AIR FRY program, and set the temperature to 180°C. Set the time to 12-15 minutes.
8. Press the START/STOP button to begin cooking.
9. After 6 minutes, carefully flip the fritters.
10. Continue cooking for another 6-9 minutes, or until the fritters are golden brown and crispy.
11. Once done, remove the Veggie Fritters from the air fryer and let them cool for a few minutes.
12. Serve the **Veggie Fritters** hot with your favorite dipping sauce or as a side dish.

Printed in Great Britain
by Amazon